Orthogonal Array

(A Statistical Tool for Software Testing)

*

by

Dr. Ramamurthy N

M.Sc., B.G.L., C.A.I.I.B., C.C.P., D.S.A.D.P., C.I.S.A., P.M.P., CGBL, 6σ-Black-Belt

&

Ravishankar R B.Tech.

*

Name of the Book:	**Orthogonal Array** (A Statistical Tool for Software Testing)
First Edition: Second Edition:	2013 2016
Authors:	Dr. **Ramamurthy N & Ravishankar R,** http://ramamurthy.jaagruti.co.in/
Copyright ©:	With **Ramamurthy N** (No part of this book may be reproduced in any manner whatsoever without the written permission).
Number of Pages:	180

*****

Table of Contents

*****

Dedication

I dedicate this book to the entire Information Technology Industry of the globe which has turned around the world and brought me to this level.

Ramamurthy N

Ln. Prof. Dr. Manivannan Sethuraman
B.Tech., D.E.M., D.T.Tech., A.M.S.P.I., M.B.A., M.S.,
P.M.P., F.M.S.P.I., Q.P.M.P., S.C.E.A, M.I.E., W.C.P.,
C.S.Q.A., F.M.I.P.M.A., S.C.J.P., F.M.I.A.E.M.E., Ph.D.
Managing Director & Chief Editorial Officer

Foreword

Software testing is an investigation conducted to provide stakeholders with information about the quality of the product or service under test. Software testing can also provide an objective, independent view of the software to allow the business to appreciate and understand the risks of software implementation. Test techniques include, but are not limited to, the process of executing a program or application with the intent of finding software bugs (errors or other defects).

However rigor testing is done, can anyone be satisfied that the software product is "100% bug free" – very difficult to certify. On the other hand there cannot a compromise on the quality of software products – especially in the mission critical applications catering to the industries like banking, finance, defense, air space, etc. At the same time how much of time, money and effort can be spent on such testing. Research/ statistics establish that 40 to 50% of the project effort is spent towards testing. There should be a balance between these two. There comes

Transstellar Journal Publications & Research Consultancy Pvt. Ltd.
Registered Office · Plot no. 35, Enginn Road, Second Class Street, Thiruvika Nagar, Perungudi, Chennai - 600 096, India, Fax · +91 - 44 - 42603609, admin@tjprc.org
Corporate Office · 151, 1st Floor, 2nd Main Road, Bhuvaneswari Nagar, Velachery, Chennai - 600 042, Tamil Nadu, India, Tel · +91-044 - 4300 2900, www.tjprc.org
· Canada   · India   · Qatar   · Singapore   · UK   · USA

Orthogonal Arrays handy.

Orthogonal Arrays (often referred as Taguchi Methods) are often employed in testing to study the effect of several control factors.

An orthogonal array is a type of experiment where the columns for the independent variables are 'orthogonal' to one another. The major benefits of using an Orthogonal Array are:

- Conclusions valid over the entire region spanned by the control factors and their settings
- Large saving in the experimental effort
- Analysis is easy

To define an orthogonal array, one must identify:

- Number of factors to be studied
- Levels for each factor
- The specific 2-factor interactions to be estimated
- The special difficulties that would be encountered in running the Experiment

To understand the construction of Orthogonal Arrays, one need to understand some statistical terms and concepts and also should have deep understanding of different testing methods and especially the complete functionality of the software product.

While the concepts of Design of Experiments and effective use of Orthogonal Array have been established in the industry, the proliferation of these techniques and usage is limited to a few instances, because of the lack of knowledge.

This book explains in simple terms the nuances of software testing and Orthogonal Array. The language is so simple that everyone can understand easily. It will serve as a step by step reference guide for the DoE and OA techniques and a ready reckoner for preparation of test cases. This will help the project managers, testers forming part of the project teams, functional testers from the user community for assessing completeness of testing, quality assurance teams and all those who are interested in testing. It also provides some simple tools for determining the optimum number of test cases without compromising on the test coverage.

It is a good idea Mr. Ramamurthy has thought of including a chapter on introducing Six Sigma, which is another scientific and statistics oriented process improvement technique. When followed in strict sense will result in cost reduction and/ or increased income.

Mr. **Ramamurthy** has lot of experience in using major banking applications and implementing software solutions as well. I know him for quite some time and he has also authored couple of religious books. His expertise and experience is visible in his writing. It is his passion towards sharing of knowledge that makes him write such book. I understand that Mr. **Ravishankar** has given the student/ reader perspective to the book and has value added a lot in bringing up this book.

Let the authors come out with more of such books for the community. I wish them all success in all their endeavors.

Sincerely,

(Manivannan Sethuraman)

MD & CEO,
www.tjprc.org

Preface

Dr. Juran, one of the quality Gurus[1], defines Quality as **"Fitness for use"**. In this context `Quality' means quality of the product or end deliverable. Testing plays a vital role in determining the **Fitness for use** and to ensure that the delivered product meets all the requirements of the users.

A study by Project Management Institute (PMI) shows that 90% of the projects executed are abandoned at various stages of completion, since they do not meet the specifications intended. Hence it is all the more important to determine the right parameters for testing with minimum effort to ensure successful project completion.

While testing is being performed for every project, the quality of testing itself is questionable. Most of the testing performed is not process oriented. In any project, as the number of variables/ inputs increases, the complexity of testing increases. Hence in the practical scenario it is almost impossible to do exhaustive testing, more so in the case of regression testing. Given the tight schedule of the software engineers and shorter developmental lifecycle of the project, the testing would become ad hoc and inefficient without proper testing methods (though ad-hoc testing is claimed to be more efficient by James Bach, there is no proper structured or formal way to test in ad-hoc and also the skill level of tester required is very high).

DOE is a formal structured and scientific technique for studying any situation that involves a response that varies as a function of one or more independent variables. DOE is specifically designed to address complex problems where more than one variable may affect a response and two or more variables may interact with each other.

---

[1] Guru is a Samskrit word, which means a teacher well versed in the subject

Orthogonal Array (OA) is a technique used for testing, derived from the concept of Design of Experiments. When used correctly, DOE and OA can provide the answers to specific questions about the behavior of a system, using minimum number of experimental observations spanning almost the entire domain. DOE and OA give the answers that we seek with a minimum expenditure of time and resources, thereby minimizing costs.

As explained by S. Hedayat, the existence of OA, a combination of various statistics application, and the effective use of it, have been established across diverse industries, the proliferation of these techniques and usage is limited to a few instances, because of the lack of knowledge of these techniques. In this book the concepts behind them are explained along with a successful application in software testing.

Our sincere thanks to Mr. Manivannan for his nice words about us and for his perfect introduction. Readers can feel free to send their feedback to the authors.

Chennai   *Ramamurthy N*
September 2013   *Ravishankar R*

*****

Chapter 1 - Software Testing

Before going in detail about software testing, a brief understanding of the component development process is required. The development process for a system is traditionally known as a **Waterfall Model** where each step follows the next, as if in a waterfall. This shows how various components of a product produced at each step are used in the process following it.

Business Case:

The first step in development is a business investigation followed by a "Business Case" produced by the customer for a system. This outlines a new system, or changes to an existing system, which it is anticipated will deliver business benefits and outlines the costs expected when developing and running the system. This is generally done through a market research or market survey.

Requirements:

The next broad step is to define a set of "Requirements", which is a statement by the customer of what the system shall achieve in order to meet the need or requirement. These involve both functional and non-functional requirements.

System Specification:

"Requirements" are then passed to developers, who produce a "System Specification". This changes the focus from what the system shall achieve to how it will be achieved by analyzing both the functional and non-functional requirements.

System Design:

Next step is to produce a "System Design" from the "System Specification". This takes the features required and maps them to various components and defines the relationships between these components. The whole design should result in a detailed system design that will achieve what is required by the "System Specification".

Component Design:

Each component then has a "Component Design", which describes in detail exactly how it will perform its piece of processing.

Component Construction:

Finally each component is built and then is ready for the test process.

WHAT IS SOFTWARE TESTING? Testing is a process of *verifying* and *validating* that the software produced whether they:

• Meet the business and technical requirements that guided its design and development and
• Work as expected.

The testing process also identifies important defects, flaws, bugs, or errors in the final product. It is "important" because defects must be categorized by severity. During test planning it would be decided what an important defect is, by reviewing the requirements and design documents with a focus towards answering the question "Important to whom?" Generally speaking, an important defect is one that from the customer's perspective affects the usability or functionality of the software application.

Testing has three main purposes: verification, validation and defect finding.

The *verification* process confirms that the software meets its technical specifications. A "specification" is a description of a function in terms of a measurable output value given a specific input value under specific preconditions.

The *validation* process confirms that the software meets the business requirements. A simple example of a business requirement is "After choosing a branch office code, information about the branch's name, customer account managers will appear in a new window. The window will present manager identification and summary information about each manager's customer base: <list of data elements>."

A **defect** is a variance between the expected and actual results The defect's ultimate source may be traced to a fault introduced in the specification, design, or development (coding) phases.

WHY SOFTWARE TESTING? Software testing is focused on finding **defects** in the final **product** while 'bug' is really a problem in the code which is not found out during software testing. One important defect that better testing would have found is:

In February 2003 the U.S. Treasury Department mailed 50,000 Social Security checks without a beneficiary name. A spokesperson said that the missing names were due to a software program maintenance error.

Software testing checks whether:

- Does it really work as expected?
- Does it meet the all the requirements of the user(s)?

- Is it what the users expect?
- Do the users like it?
- Is it compatible with other systems?
- How does it perform?
- How does it scale when more users are added during expansion?
- Which areas need more work?
- Is it ready for release?

What can be done with the answers to these questions?

- Save time and money by identifying defects early
- Avoid or reduce development downtime
- Provide better customer service by building a better application
- Know that the users have satisfied with the requirements
- Build a list of desired modifications and enhancements for later versions
- Identify and catalog reusable modules and components
- Identify areas where programmers and developers need training

WHAT IS TO BE TESTED? First, test what's important. Focus on the core functionality - the parts that are critical or popular - before looking at the 'nice to have' features. Concentrate on the application's capabilities in common usage situations before going on to unlikely/ extreme situations. For instance, if the application retrieves data and performance are important, test reasonable queries with a normal load on the server before going on to unlikely ones at peak usage times. It is worth repetition: "focus on what's important". Good business requirements will tell us what's important. The value of software testing is that it goes far beyond testing the underlying code. It also examines the functional behavior of the application. Behavior is a function of the code, but it does not always follow that if the behaviour is 'bad' then the code is bad. It is entirely possible that the code is solid but the requirements were inaccurately or incompletely collected and communicated. It is entirely possible that the application can be doing exactly what it has been told to do but it has not been told to do the right thing. A comprehensive testing regime examines all components associated with the application. Even more, testing provides an opportunity to validate and verify things like the assumptions that went into the requirements, the appropriateness of the systems that the application is to run on and the manuals and documentations that accompany the application.

Testing can involve some or all of the following factors. The more, the better:

- Business requirements
- Functional design requirements
- Technical design requirements
- Regulatory requirements
- Programmer code
- System administration standards and restrictions
- Corporate standards
- Professional or trade association best practices
- Hardware configuration
- Cultural issues and language differences

WHO DOES THE TESTING? Software testing is not a one person job. It takes a team, but the team may be larger or smaller depending on the size and complexity of the application being tested. The programmer(s) who wrote the application should have a reduced role in the testing, as far as possible. In other words the testing team should be independent of the developing team. The concern here is that they're already so intimately involved with the product and 'know' that it works that they may not be able to take an unbiased look at the results of their efforts. The testers must be cautious, curious, critical but non-judgmental and good communicators. One part of their job is to ask questions that the developers might find not be able to ask themselves or are awkward, irritating, insulting or even threatening to the developers.

- How well does it work?
- What does it mean that "it works"?
- How can it be known that it works? What evidences are available?
- In what ways could it seem to work but still have something wrong?
- In what ways could it seem to not work but really be working?
- What might cause it to not to work well?

A good developer does not necessarily make a good tester and vice versa, but testers and developers do share at least one major trait - they itch to get their hands on the keyboard. As laudable as this may be, being in a hurry to start can cause important design work to be glossed over and so special, subtle situations might be missed that would otherwise be identified in planning. Like code reviews, test design reviews are a good sanity check and well worth the time and effort. Testers are the only people who will use the system as heavily an expert user on the business side. User testing almost invariably recruits too many novice business users because they're available and the application must be usable by them. The problem is that novices do not have the business experience that the expert users have and might not recognize that something is wrong. Testers must find the defects that only the expert users will find because the experts may not report problems if they've learned that it is not worth their time or trouble.

Table 1: Key Players and Their Roles:

Player	Key Roles
Business sponsor(s) and partners	Provides funding Specifies requirements and deliverables Approves changes and some test results
Project Manager	Plans and manages the project
Software Developer(s)	Designs, codes and builds the application Participates in code reviews and testing Fixes bugs, defects and shortcomings
Testing Coordinator(s)	Creates test plans and test specifications based on the requirements
Functional and technical Tester(s)	Executes the tests and documents results

The V-Model of Software Testing:

Software testing is too important to leave it to the end of the project and the V-Model of incorporates testing throughout the software development life cycle. In a diagram of the V-Model, the V proceeds down and then up, from left to right depicting the basic sequence of development and testing activities. The model highlights the existence of different levels of testing and depicts the way each relates to a different phase. Like any model, the V-Model has detractors and arguably has deficiencies and alternatives but it clearly illustrates that testing can and should start at the very beginning of the project. In the requirements gathering stage the business requirements can verify and validate the business case used to justify the project. The business requirements are used to guide the user acceptance testing. The model illustrates how each subsequent phase should verify and validate work done in the previous phase and how work done during development is used to guide the individual testing phases. Application testing begins with Unit Testing and each of these test phases has been discussed in detail in the section titled "Types of Tests".

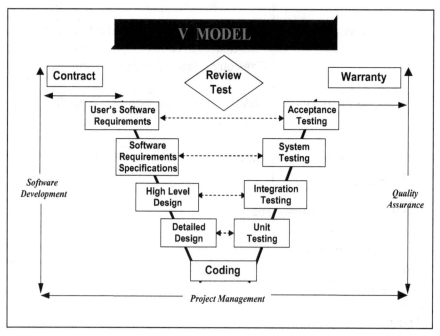

Figure 1: The V-Model of Software Testing

1.1 The Test Plan

The test plan is a mandatory document. The testing cannot be done without a plan. For simple, straight-forward projects the plan need not has to be elaborate but it must address certain items. As identified by the "American National Standards Institute and Institute for Electrical and Electronic Engineers (IEEE) Standard 829/1983 for Software Test Documentation", the following components should be covered in a software test plan:

Table 2: Components of a software test plan

Component	Description	Purpose
Responsibilities	Specific people and their assignments	Assigns responsibilities and keeps everyone on track and focused
Assumptions	Code and systems status and availability	Avoids misunderstandings about schedules
Test	Testing scope, schedule, duration and prioritization	Outlines the entire process and maps specific tests
Communication	Communications plan — who, what, when, how	Everyone knows what they need to know when they need to know it
Risk Analysis	Critical items that will be tested	Provides focus by identifying areas that are critical for success
Defect Reporting	How defects will be logged and documented	Tells how to document a defect so that it can be reproduced, fixed and retested
Environment	The technical environment, data, work area and interfaces used in testing	Reduces or eliminates misunderstandings and sources of potential delay

REDUCE RISK WITH A TEST PLAN: The release of a new application or an upgrade inherently carries a certain amount of risk that it will fail to do what it is supposed to do. A good test plan goes a long way towards reducing this risk. By identifying areas that are riskier than others the team can concentrate the testing efforts there. These areas include not only the must-have features but also areas in which the technical staff is less experienced. Because riskier areas require more certainty that they work properly, failing to correctly identify those risky areas leads to a misallocated testing effort.

How to identify risky areas? Ask everyone for their opinion! Gather information from developers, sales and marketing staff, technical writers, customer support people and of course any users who are available. Historical metrics and bug and testing reports from similar products or previous releases will identify areas to explore. Bug reports from customers are important, but also bugs reported by the developers themselves need to be looked into. These will provide insight to the technical areas they may be having trouble in.

Types of defects: When the problems are inevitably found, it is important that both the IT and the business users have previously agreed on how to respond. This includes having a method for rating the importance of defects so that defect-fixing work can be focused on the most important problems. It is very common to use a set of rating categories that represent decreasing relative severity in terms of business/ commercial impact. In one system, '1' is the most severe and `6' has the least impact. It has to be kept in mind that an ordinal system does not allow an average score to be calculated, but it should not need to do that anyway - a defect's category should be pretty obvious: For e.g.:

1. **Show Stopper** – It is impossible to continue running the application because of the severity of the defect.
2. **Critical** – Testing can continue but the application cannot be released into production until this defect is fixed.

3. **Major** – Testing can continue but this defect will result in a severe departure from the business requirements, if released for production.
4. **Medium** – Testing can continue and the defect will cause only minimal departure from the business requirements, when in production.
5. **Minor** – Testing can continue and the defect will not affect the release into production. The defect should be corrected but little or no changes to business requirements are envisaged.
6. **Cosmetic** – Minor cosmetic issues like colors, fonts and pitch size that do not affect testing or production release. If, however, these features are important business requirements then they will receive a higher severity level.

WHAT SHOULD A TEST PLAN TEST? Testing experts generally agree that test plans are often biased towards functional testing during which each feature is tested alone in a unit test and that the systems integration test is just a series of unit tests strung together. The problem that this approach causes is that if each feature is tested alone and then string a bunch of these tests together, one can never find that a series of steps such as open a document, edit the document, print the document, save the document, edit one page, print one page, save as a new document does not work. But a user will find out and probably quickly. Admittedly, testing every combination of keystrokes or commands is difficult at best and may well be impossible (this is where unstructured testing comes in), but it must be remembered that features do not function in isolation from each other.

Users have a task orientation: To find the defects that they will find - the ones that are important to them - test plans need to be exercised the application across functional areas by mimicking both typical and a typical user tasks. A test like the sequence is called scenario testing, task-based testing, or use-case testing.

An incomplete test plan can result in a failure to check how the application works on different hardware and operating systems or when combined with different third-party software. This is not always needed but the customers will want to think about the equipment they use. There may be more than a few possible system combinations that need to be tested and that can require a possibly expensive computer lab stocked with hardware and spending much time setting up tests. Configuration testing is not cheap, but it is worth it when the application running on the standard in-house platform which "entirely conforms to industry standards" behaves differently when it runs on the boxes the customers are using. In a 1996 incident, the development and testing was done on new 386-class machines and the application worked just fine. Not until customers complained about performance issues till the development team learnt that they were using 286's with slow hard drives.

A crucial test is to see how the application behaves when it is under a normal load and then under stress. The definition of stress, of course, will be derived from the business requirements, but for a web-enabled application stress could be caused by a spike in the number of transactions, a few very large transactions at the same time, or a large number of almost identical simultaneous transactions. The goal is to see what happens when the application is pushed to substantially more than the basic requirements. **Stress testing** is often put off until the end of testing, after everything else that is going to be fixed has been. Unfortunately that leaves little time for repairs when the requirements specify 40 concurrent users and it is found that performance becomes unacceptable at 50. Finally, two more major common omissions in many test plans - the installation procedures and the documentation are ignored. Everyone has tried to follow installation instructions that were missing a key step or two and have all paged through incomprehensible documentation. Although those documents may have been written by a professional technical writer, they probably were not tested in a real environment. Bad installation instructions immediately cause lowered expectations of what to expect from the product and poorly organized or written documentation certainly does not help a confused or irritated customer feel better. Testing installation procedures and documentation is a good way to avoid making a bad first impression or making a bad situation worse.

Definition of some important concepts relating to testing follows:

Test Plan: A formal detailed document that describes:

- Scope, objectives and the approach to testing,
- People and equipment dedicated/ allocated to testing
- Tools that will be used
- Dependencies and risks
- Categories of defects
- Test entry and exit criteria
- Measurements to be captured
- Reporting and communication processes
- Schedules and milestones

Test Case: A document that defines a test item and specifies a set of test inputs or data, execution conditions and expected results. The inputs/ data used by a test case should be both normal and intended to produce a 'good' result and intentionally erroneous and intended to produce an error. A test case is generally executed manually but many test cases can be combined for automated execution.

Test Script: Step-by-step procedures for using a test case to test a specific unit of code, function, or capability.

Test Scenario: A chronological record of the details of the execution of a test script. It captures the specifications, tester activities and outcomes and is used to identify defects.

Test Run: A series of logically related groups of test cases or conditions.

*****

Chapter 2 - Types of Software Tests

As the project team gets involved in the development of a new system a vast number of software tests appear to be required to prove the system. While they are consistent in all having the word "test" in them, their relative importance to each other is not clear.

A very broad classification of software testing methods is:

Static Testing:

The verification activities fall into the category of Static Testing. During static testing, the testers have a checklist to check whether the work they are doing is going as per the set standards of the organization. These standards can be for Coding, Integrating and Deployment. Reviews, Inspections and Walkthroughs are various static testing methodologies.

Dynamic Testing:

Dynamic Testing involves working with the software, giving input values and checking if the output is behaving as expected. These are the validation activities. Unit Tests, Integration Tests, System Tests and Acceptance Tests are few of the Dynamic Testing methodologies.

Software testing can further be classified into *formal* and *less formal* type of testing. Under the classification of **formal** type of software testing the following methods are widely in use:

- Component.
- Interface.
- System.
- Acceptance.

- Release.

Under **less formal** type the major testing methods are:

- Ad-Hoc Experimentation.
- Exploratory.
- Improvisational.

The level of test is the primary focus of a system and derives from the way a software system is designed and built up. As introduced earlier, conventionally this is known as the "V" model, which maps the types of test to each stage of development. The V-Model of testing identifies five software testing phases, each with a certain type of test associated with it. Various such tests and the corresponding phases are:

- Development Phase - Technical Design - Unit Testing
- System Integration Phase - Functional Design - System Testing and Integration Testing,
- User Acceptance Phase - Business Requirements - User Acceptance Testing
- Implementation Phase - Business Case - Product Verification Testing

2.1 Formal Testing Methods

Some of the formal testing methods are discussed here alongwith entry and exit criteria for each of the methods.

2.1.1   Unit Testing

This is also sometimes called as **Component Testing.** It is a series of stand-alone tests, which are conducted during or at the end of development of each of the modules, by the developers. Each test examines an individual component that is new or has been modified. A unit test is also called a module test because it tests the individual modules of code that comprise the application. Each test validates a single module that, based on the technical design documents, was built to perform a certain task with the expectation that it will behave in a specific way or produce specific results. Unit tests focus on functionality and reliability and the entry and exit criteria can be the same for each module or specific to a particular module. Unit testing is done in a test environment prior to system integration testing. If a defect is discovered during a unit test, the severity of the defect will dictate whether or not it will be fixed before the module is approved. Sample Entry and Exit Criteria for Unit Testing:

Entry Criteria for unit testing:

- Business Requirements are at least 80% complete and have been approved to-date
- Technical Design has been finalized and approved
- Development environment has been established and is stable
- Code development for the module is complete

Exit Criteria for unit testing:

- Code has version control in place
- No known major or critical defects prevents any modules from moving to System Testing
- A testing transition meeting has been held and the developers signed off
- Approval of the Project Manager has been obtained

2.1.2   System Testing

System Testing tests all components and modules that are new, changed, affected by a change, or needed to form the complete application. The system test may require involvement of other systems but this should be minimized as much as possible to reduce the risk of externally - induced bugs/ issues.

The emphasis in system testing is validating and verifying the functional design specification and seeing how all the modules work together. The first system test is often a *smoke test*. This is an informal quick-and-dirty run through of the application's major functions without bothering with details. The term comes from the hardware testing practice of turning on a new piece of equipment for the first time and considering it a success if it does not start smoking or burst into flame. System testing requires many test runs because it entails feature by feature validation of behavior using a wide range of both normal and erroneous test inputs and data. When an error or defect is discovered, previously executed system tests must be re-run after the repair is made to make sure that the modifications did not cause other problems.

Once the entire system has been built then it has to be tested against the "System Specification" to check if it delivers the features required. It is still developer focused, although specialist developers known as systems testers are normally employed to do it.

In essence System Testing is not about checking the individual parts of the design, but about checking the system as a whole. In effect it is one giant component.

System testing can involve a number of specialist types of tests to see if all the functional and non-functional requirements have been met.

In addition to functional requirements these may include the following types of testing of the non-functional requirements:

- Performance - Are the performance criteria met?
- Volume - Can large volumes of information be handled?
- Stress - Can peak volumes of information be handled?
- Documentation - Is the documentation usable for the system?
- Robustness - Does the system remain stable under adverse circumstances?

Sample Entry and Exit Criteria for System Testing:

Entry Criteria for System Testing:

- Unit testing for each module has been completed and approved;
- Each module is under version control
- An incident tracking plan has been approved
- A system testing environment has been established
- The system testing schedule is approved and in place

Exit Criteria for System Testing:

- Application meets all documented business and functional requirements
- No known critical defects prevent moving to the next stage
- All stakeholders have approved the completed tests
- A testing transition meeting has been held and the developers signed off

As a part of system testing, **conformance tests** and reviews can be run to verify that the application conforms to corporate or industry standards in terms of portability, interoperability and compliance with standards. For example, to enhance application portability a corporate standard may be that SQL queries must be written so that they work against any database.

2.1.3   Integration Testing

This is also sometimes called as **Interface Testing**. As the components are constructed and tested they are then linked together to check if they work with each other. It is a fact that two components that have passed all their tests individually, when connected to each other produce one new component full of faults. These tests can be done by specialists, or by the developers.

Integration testing examines all the components and modules that are new, modified, affected by a change, or needed to form a complete system. This testing is more important where there are other systems interfacing with the current system either inwardly or outwardly. Where System Testing tries to minimize the outside factors, Integration Testing requires involvement of other systems and interfaces with other applications, including those owned by an outside vendor, external partner(s), or the customer. For example, Integration Testing for a new web interface that collects user input for addition to a database must include the database's ETL application even if the database is hosted by a vendor - the complete system must be tested end-to-end. In this example, Integration Testing does not stop with the database load; test reads must verify that it was correctly loaded. Integration Testing also differs from System Testing in that when a defect is discovered, not all previously executed tests have to be re-run after the fixing is done. Only those tests with a connection to the defect must be re-run, but retesting must start at the point of repair, if it is before the point of failure. For example, the retest of a failed FTP process may use an existing data file instead of recreating it, if up to that point everything else was OK.

Integration Testing is not focused on what the components are doing but on how they communicate with each other, as specified in the "System Design". The "System Design" defines relationships between components and this involves stating:

- What a component can expect from another component in terms of services.
- How these services will be asked for.
- How they will be given.
- How to handle non-standard conditions, i.e. errors.

Sample Entry and Exit Criteria for Integration Testing:

Entry Criteria for Integrations Testing:

- System Testing has been completed and signed off
- Outstanding issues and defects have been identified and documented
- Test scripts and schedule are ready
- The Integration Testing environment is established

Exit Criteria for Integration Testing:

- All systems involved passed Integration Testing and meet agreed upon functionality and performance requirements
- Outstanding defects have been identified, documented and presented to the business sponsor
- Stress, performance and load tests have been satisfactorily conducted
- The implementation plan is final draft stage
- A testing transition meeting has been held and everyone has signed off

Integration Testing has a number of sub-types of tests that may or may not be used, depending on the application being tested or expected usage patterns.

Compatibility Testing: Compatibility tests insure that the application works with differently configured systems based on what the users have or may have. When testing a web interface, this means testing for compatibility with different types of browsers and connection speeds.

Performance Testing – Performance tests are used to evaluate and understand the application's scalability when, for example, more users are added or the volume of data increases. This is particularly important for identifying bottlenecks in high usage applications. The basic approach is to collect timings of the critical business processes while the test system is under a very low load (a 'quiet box' condition) and then collect the same timings with progressively higher loads until the maximum required load is reached. For data retrieval application, reviewing the performance pattern may show that a change needs to be made in a stored SQL procedure or that an index should be added to the database design.

Stress Testing – Stress Testing is Performance Testing at higher than normal simulated loads. Stressing runs the system or application beyond the limits of its specified requirements to determine the load under which it fails and how it fails. A gradual performance slow-down leading to a non-catastrophic system halt is the desired result, but if the system will suddenly crash and burn, it is important to know the point where that happens. Catastrophic failure in production means beepers going off, people coming in after hours, system restarts, frayed tempers and possible financial losses. This test is arguably the most important test for mission - critical systems.

Load Testing – Load Tests are a little different from Stress Tests. They test the capability of the application to function properly under expected normal production conditions and measure the response times for critical transactions or processes to determine if they are within limits specified in the business requirements and design documents or that they meet defined Service Level Agreements (SLA). For database applications, load testing must be executed on a current production - size database. If some database tables are forecast to grow much larger in the foreseeable future then serious consideration should be given to testing against a database of the projected size.

Performance, stress and load testing are all major undertakings and will require substantial input from the business sponsors and IT staff in setting up a test environment and designing test cases that can be accurately executed. Because of this, these tests are sometimes delayed and done parallel to the User Acceptance Testing phase. Load tests especially must be documented in detail so that the tests are repeatable in case they need to be executed several times to ensure that new releases or changes in database size do not push response times beyond prescribed requirements and Service Level Agreements.

2.1.4   User Acceptance Testing (UAT)

User Acceptance Testing is also called **Beta testing or application testing or end-user testing**. Whatever way it is called, it is where testing moves from the hands of the IT department into those of the business users. Software vendors often make extensive use of Beta testing, some more formally than others, because they can get users to do it for free. By the time UAT is ready to start, the IT staff has resolved in one way or other all the defects they identified. Regardless of their best efforts, though, they probably do not find all the flaws in the application. A general rule of thumb is that no matter how bulletproof an application seems when it goes into UAT, a user somewhere can still find a sequence of commands that will produce an error. To be of real use, UAT cannot be random users playing with the application. A mix of business users with varying degrees of experience and subject matter expertise need to actively participate in a controlled environment. Representatives from the group work with Testing Coordinators to design and conduct tests that reflect activities and conditions seen in normal business usage.

Acceptance Testing checks the system against the "Requirements". It is similar to systems testing in that the whole system is checked but the important difference is the change in focus:

System Testing checks that the system that was specified has been delivered.

Acceptance Testing checks that the system delivers what was requested.

The customer and not the developer normally execute the acceptance testing. The customer knows what is required from the system to achieve value in the business and is the only person qualified to make that judgment.

Business users also participate in evaluating the results. This insures that the application is tested in real-world environment and that the tests cover the full range of business usage. The goal of UAT is to simulate realistic business activity and processes in the test environment. A phase of UAT called **"Unstructured testing"** will be conducted whether or not it is in the Test Plan. Also known as **guerilla testing**, this is when business users bash away at the keyboard to find the weakest parts of the application. In effect, they try to break it. Although it is a free-form test, it is important that users who participate, understand that they have to be able to reproduce the steps that led to any errors they find. Otherwise it is of no use. A common occurrence in UAT is that once the business users start working with the application they find that it does not do exactly what they want it to do or that it does something that, although correct, is not quite optimal. Investigation finds that the root cause is in the Business Requirements and hence the users will seek ask for a change in the application. During UAT, the change control must be most seriously enforced. In other words scope creep is especially dangerous in this late phase and must be avoided.

Sample Entry and Exit Criteria for User Acceptance Testing:

Entry Criteria for UAT:

- Integration testing signoff was obtained
- Business requirements have been met or renegotiated with the Business Sponsor or representative(s).
- UAT test scripts are ready for execution
- The testing environment is established
- Security requirements have been documented and necessary user access obtained

Exit Criteria for UAT:

- UAT has been completed and approved by the user community in a transition meeting
- Change control is managing requested modifications and enhancements
- Business sponsor agrees that known defects do not impact a production release - no remaining defects are rated 3, 2, or 1

2.1.5   Production Verification Testing

Production Verification Testing is a final opportunity to determine if the software is ready for release. Its purpose is to simulate the production cutover as closely as possible and for a period of time simulate real business activity. As a sort of full dress rehearsal, it should identify anomalies or unexpected changes to existing processes introduced by the new application. For mission critical applications the importance of this testing cannot be overstated. The application should be completely removed from the test environment and then completely reinstalled exactly as it will be in the production implementation. Then mock production runs will verify that the existing business process flows, interfaces and batch processes continue to run correctly and as expected. Unlike **parallel testing**, mock processing may not provide accurate data handling results due to limitations of the testing database or the source data.

Sample Entry and Exit Criteria for Production Verification Testing:

Entry Criteria for Production Verification Testing:

- UAT has been completed and approved by all the stakeholders
- Known defects have been documented
- Migration package documentation has been completed, reviewed and approved by the production systems manager

Exit Criteria for Production Verification Testing:

- Package migration is complete
- Installation testing has been performed and documented and the results have been signed off
- Mock testing has been documented, reviewed and approved

- All tests show that the application will not adversely affect the production environment
- A System Change Record with approvals has been prepared

2.1.6   Parallel Testing

Parallel Testing is that the old and new systems are run side-by-side. If it is first time application, then the manual and the application are run in parallel. The results, reports, etc., from the old and the new systems are compared for consistency. Once the users are satisfied with the new system, the old system is retired and the new system moved to production.

Sample Entry and Exit Criteria for Parallel Testing:

Entry Criteria for Parallel Testing – this would be similar to that of Production Verification Testing:

- UAT testing has been completed and approved by all necessary parties
- Known defects have been documented
- Migration package documentation has been completed, reviewed and approved by the production systems manager
- The required master and other transaction data are replicated from the old system

Exit Criteria for Parallel Testing:

- All the outputs of the new system has been compared, controlled and verified to the utmost satisfaction of the users.
- The new system is moved to production environment
- The old system is retired

2.1.7   Regression Testing

Regression testing is also known as **validation testing** and provides a consistent, repeatable validation of each change to an application under development or being modified. Bugs are likely to appear in one part of a working program immediately after an 'unrelated' part of the program is modified. Each time a defect is fixed, the potential exists to inadvertently introduce new errors, problems and defects. An element of uncertainty is introduced about ability of the application to repeat everything that went right up to the point of failure. Regression testing is the probably selective retesting of an application or system that has been modified to insure that no previously working components, functions, or features fail as a result of the repairs. Regression testing is conducted in parallel with other tests and can be viewed as a quality control tool to ensure that the newly modified code still complies with its specified requirements and that unmodified code has not been affected by the change. It is important to understand that regression testing does not test that a specific defect has been fixed. Regression testing tests that the rest of the application up to the point or repair was not adversely affected by the fix.

Sample Entry and Exit Criteria for Regression Testing:

Entry Criteria for Regression Testing:

- The defect is repeatable and has been properly documented
- A change control or defect tracking record was opened to identify and track the regression testing effort
- A regression test specific to the defect has been created, reviewed and accepted

Exit Criteria for Regression Testing:

- Results of the test show no negative impact to the application

Release Testing: Even if a system meets all its requirements, there is still a case to be answered that it will benefit the business. The linking of "Business Case" to Release Testing is looser than the others, but is still important.

Release Testing is about seeing if the new or changed system will work in the existing business environment. Mainly this means the technical environment and checks concerns such as:

- Does it affect any other systems running on the hardware?
- Is it compatible with other systems?
- Does it have acceptable performance under load?

These tests are usually run the by the computer operations team in a business. The answers to their questions could have significant a financial impact if new computer hardware should be required and adversely affect the "Business Case".

It would appear obvious that the operations team should be involved right from the start of a project to give their opinion of the impact a new system may have. They could then make sure the "Business Case" is relatively sound, at least from the capital expenditure and ongoing running costs aspects. However in practice many operations teams only find out about project just weeks before it is supposed to go live, which can result in major problems.

2.1.8   Functional Testing

Validating an application whether it conforms to its specifications and correctly performs all its required functions is called Functional Testing. This entails a series of tests which perform a feature by feature validation of behavior, using a wide range of normal and erroneous input data. This can involve testing of the product's user interface, APIs, database management, security, installation, networking, etc. Functional testing can be performed on an automated or manual basis using black box or white box methodologies.

2.1.9   Black Box Testing

Black-box and white-box are test design methods. Black-box test design treats the system as a "black-box", so it does not explicitly use knowledge of the internal structure. Black-box test design is usually described as focusing on testing functional requirements. Synonyms for black-box include: **behavioral, functional, opaque-box** and **closed-box**. White-box test design allows one to peek inside the 'box' and it focuses specifically on using internal knowledge of the software programs to guide the selection of test data. Synonyms for white-box include: **structural, glass-box** and **clear-box**.

Black box testing attempts to derive sets of inputs that will fully exercise all the functional requirements of a system. This type of testing attempts to find errors in the following categories:

- Incorrect or missing functions
- Interface errors
- Errors in data structures or external database access
- Performance errors and
- Initialization and termination errors.

Tests are designed to answer the following questions:

- How is the function's validity tested?
- What classes of input will make good test cases?

- Is the system particularly sensitive to certain input values?
- How are the boundaries of a data class isolated?
- What data rates and data volume can the system tolerate?
- What effect will specific combinations of data have on system operation?

Black Box testing tends to be applied during later stages of the Testing Process. Test cases should be derived which reduce the number of additional test cases that must be designed to achieve reasonable testing and it should also tell something about the presence or absence of classes of errors, rather than an error associated only with the specific test at hand.

The different Methods of Black Box Testing are:

Equivalence Partitioning: This method divides the input domain of a program into classes of data from which test cases can be derived. Equivalence partitioning strives to define a test case that uncovers classes of errors and thereby reduces the number of test cases needed. It is based on an evaluation of equivalence classes for an input condition. An equivalence class represents a set of valid or invalid states for input conditions.

Equivalence classes may be defined according to the following guidelines:

- If an input condition specifies a range, then one valid and two invalid equivalence classes are defined.
- If an input condition requires a specific value, then one valid and two invalid equivalence classes are defined.
- If an input condition specifies a member of a set, then one valid and one invalid equivalence classes are defined.

- If an input condition is Boolean, then one valid and one invalid equivalence class are defined.

Boundary Value Analysis (BVA): This method leads to a selection of test cases that exercise boundary values. It complements equivalence partitioning since it selects test cases at the edges of a class. Rather than focusing on input conditions solely, BVA derives test cases from the output domain also. BVA may be defined according to the following guidelines:

- For input values ranging between A and B, test cases should include values A, B and just above and just below A and B respectively.
- If an input condition specifies a number of values, test cases should be developed to exercise the minimum and maximum numbers and values just above and below these limits.
- Apply guidelines 1 and 2 to the output.
- If internal data structures have prescribed boundaries, a test case should be designed to exercise the data structure at its boundary.

Cause-Effect Graphing Techniques: Cause-effect graphing is a technique that provides a concise representation of logical conditions and corresponding actions. There are four steps:

- Causes (input conditions) and effects (actions) are listed for a module and an identifier is assigned to each
- A cause-effect graph is developed
- The graph is converted to a decision table
- Decision table rules are converted to test cases.

2.1.10 White Box Testing

White box testing is a test case design method that uses the control structure of the procedural design to derive test cases.
Test cases can be derived that:

- Guarantee that all independent paths within a module have been exercised at least once
- Exercise all logical decisions on their true and false sides
- Execute all loops at their boundaries and within their operational bounds
- Exercise internal data structures to ensure their validity.

2.1.11 The Nature of Software Defects

Logic errors and incorrect assumptions are inversely proportional to the probability that a program path will be executed. General processing tends to be well understood while special case processing tends to be prone to errors.

We often believe that a logical path is likely to be executed on a regular basis. Our unconscious assumptions about control flow and data lead to design errors that can only be detected by path testing.

The different White Box testing methods are:

Basis Path Testing: This method enables the designer to derive a logical complexity measure of a procedural design and use it as a guide for defining a basis set of execution paths. Test cases that exercise the basis set are guaranteed to execute every statement in the program at least once during testing.

Flow Graphs: Flow graphs can be used to represent control flow in a program and can help in the derivation of the basis set. Each flow graph node represents one or more procedural statements. The edges between nodes represent flow of control. An edge must terminate at a node, even if the node does not represent any useful procedural statements. A region in a flow graph is an area bounded by edges and nodes. Each node that contains a condition is called a predicate node. Cyclamate complexity is a metric that provides a quantitative measure of the logical complexity of a program. It defines the number of independent paths in the basis set and thus provides an upper bound for the number of tests that must be performed.

The Basis Set: An independent path is any path through a program that introduces at least one new set of processing statements (must move along at least one new edge in the path). The basis set is not unique. Any number of different basis sets can be derived for a given procedural design.

2.1.12 Deriving Test Cases

1. From the design or source code, derive a flow graph.
2. Determine the cyclamate complexity of this flow graph. Even without a flow graph, V(G) can be determined by counting the number of conditional statements in the code.
3. Determine a basis set of linearly independent paths. Predicate nodes are useful for determining the necessary paths.
4. Prepare test cases that will force execution of each path in the basis set.
5. Each test case is executed and compared to the expected results.

2.1.13 Automating Basis Set Derivation

The derivation of the flow graph and the set of basis paths is amenable to automation. A software tool to do this can be developed using a data structure called a graph matrix. A graph matrix is a square matrix whose size is equivalent to the number of nodes in the flow graph. Each row and column corresponds to a particular node and the matrix corresponds to the connections (edges) between nodes. By adding a link weight to each matrix entry, more information about the control flow can be captured. In its simplest form, the link weight is 1 if an edge exists and 0 if it does not. But other types of link weights can be represented:

- Probability that an edge will be executed
- Processing time expended during link traversal
- Memory required during link traversal
- Resources required during link traversal.

Graph theory algorithms can be applied to these graph matrices to help in the analysis necessary to produce the basis set.

Loop Testing: This white box technique focuses exclusively on the validity of loop constructs. Four different classes of loops can be defined:

- Simple loops
- Nested loops
- Concatenated loops
- Unstructured loops

Simple Loops:

The following test scenarios should be applied to simple loops where n is the maximum number of allowable passes through the loop:

1. Skip the loop entirely,
2. Only pass once through the loop,

3. M passes through the loop where m < n,

4. n - 1, n, n + 1 passes through the loop.

Nested Loops:

The testing of nested loops cannot simply extend the technique of simple loops since this would result in a geometrically increasing number of test cases. One approach for nested loops:

1. Start at the innermost loop. Set all other loops to minimum values.
2. Conduct simple loop tests for the innermost loop while holding the outer loops at their minimums.
3. Add tests for out-of-range or excluded values.
4. Work outward, conducting tests for the next loop while keeping all other outer loops at minimums and other nested loops to typical values.
5. Continue until all loops have been tested.

Concatenated Loops:

Concatenated loops can be tested as simple loops, if each loop is independent of the others. If they are not independent (e.g. the loop counter for one is the loop counter for the other), then the nested approach can be used.

Other white box testing techniques include:

- **Condition testing:** Exercises the logical conditions in a program.
- **Data flow testing**: Selects test paths according to the locations of definitions and uses of variables in the program.

While black-box and white-box are terms that are still in popular use, many people prefer the terms 'behavioral' and 'structural'.

Behavioral test design is slightly different from black-box test design because the use of internal knowledge is not strictly forbidden, but it is still discouraged.

In practice, it has not yet been adequately proven useful to use a single test design method. One has to use a prudent blend of different methods so that they are not hindered by the limitations of a particular method. Some call this **"grey-box"** or **"translucent-box"** test design.

Error Handling Testing: Error handling testing determines the ability of applications system to process the incorrect transactions properly. Errors encompass all unexpected conditions. In some systems approximately 50% of programming effort will be devoted to handling error condition.

The main objective of this testing method is to determine an application system which recognizes all expected error conditions, determine accountability of processing errors, provide procedures that have a high probability of properly correcting errors and during correction process a reasonable control is maintained over errors. Method of using it:

A group of knowledgeable people is required to anticipate what can go wrong in the application system.

It is needed that all the application knowledgeable people assemble to integrate their knowledge of user area, auditing and error tracking.

Then logical test error conditions should be created based on this assimilated information.

Example test situation:

Create a set of erroneous transactions and enter them into the application system then find out whether the system is able to identify the problems.

Using iterative testing, enter transactions and trap the errors. Correct the errors and then enter transactions with errors, which were not present in the system earlier.

Manual Support Testing: It involves testing of all the functions performed by people while preparing data and also the functions using these data.

The main objectives are to verify whether manual support documents and procedures are correct, determine manual support responsibility is correct, determine manual support people are adequately trained and determine Manual support and automated segment are properly interfaced.

Testing Process:

Process evaluated in all segments of Software Development Life Cycle (SDLC).

Execution can be done in conjunction with normal system testing.

Instead of preparing, execution and entering actual test transactions the clerical and supervisory personnel can use the results of processing from application system.

Proper Usage:

- Verification that manual systems function properly should be conducted throughout the SDLC.
- Should not be done at later stages of SDLC.

- Best done at installation stage so that the clerical people do not get used to the actual system just before system goes to production.

Mock Test Method:

Provide input personnel with the type of information they would normally receive from their customers and then have them transcribe that information and enter it in the computer.

Users can be provided a series of test conditions and then asked to respond to those conditions. Conducted in this manner, manual support testing is like an examination in which the users are asked to obtain the answer from the procedures and manuals available to them.

Intersystem Testing: This type of testing is done to ensure the interconnection between application functions correctly or properly.

The main objectives of this testing method are:

- To determine whether proper parameters and data are passed between the applications
- Documentation for the involved system is correct and accurate.
- To ensure proper timing and coordination of functions exists between the application systems.

Methodology:

Operations of multiple systems are tested.

Multiple systems are run from one another to check whether they are acceptable and are processed properly.

Conditions or environment to use this test:

- When there is change in parameters in application system
- The risk associated with erroneous parameters would decide the type of testing and extent of testing.
- Intersystem parameters would be checked or verified after the change or new application is placed in the production.

Different Instances of using this Test:

Developing test transaction set in one application and passing it to another system to verify the processing.

Entering test transactions in live production environment and then using integrated test facility to check the processing from one system to another.

Verifying new changes of the parameters in the system, which are being tested, are corrected in the document.

The major disadvantages of using this method are:

- Time consuming and tedious if test automation is not done
- Expensive if system is run several times iteratively.

2.2 Less Formal Testing Methods

Some of the informal or less formal testing methods are discussed here:

2.2.1   Ad-hoc Testing

Ad-hoc tests are one-off tests and it is a special type of exploratory test which is an informal type of testing. While formal tests put a premium on repeatability and test automation, in Ad-hoc testing it is more of exploring the causes for fault and improvising the solution for it. Much of the software industry overemphasizes the design and re-running of regression tests, at the risk of failing to run enough new tests. But the type of testing is purely dependent on the problem. For example, if the tester is working with life-critical software, there are important ethical and legal reasons for placing such a heavy emphasis on regression testing.

Here are a few excerpts about Exploratory testing:

"At some point, the tester will stop formally planning and documenting new tests until the next test cycle. But still he can keep testing and run new tests as he thinks of them, without spending much time preparing or explaining the tests. He has to trust his instincts. In this example, he quickly reached the switch point from formal to informal testing because the program crashed so soon. Something may be fundamentally wrong. If so, the program will be redesigned. Creating new test series now is risky. They may become obsolete with the next version of the program. Rather than gambling away the planning time, try some exploratory tests – whatever comes to mind".

The various elements associated with Exploratory Testing:

- It is an interweaving of test design and test execution. This is in contrast to a process in which the tests are all designed first and then run later.
- The tester learns about the product by testing it.

- An emphasis is laid on creativity and spontaneity.
- In some cases testing thus some parts of test planning.

Ad-hoc testing is a special case of Exploratory Testing. In the course of doing Exploratory Testing, many of the test cases will be ad-hoc (one-off tests), but some cases will not be. One way to distinguish between the two is to look at the notes associated with a given exploratory test. In general, exploratory tests have little or no formal documentation, but result in more informal notes. If the notes are detailed enough that the test could be re-run by reading them, then that is less likely to be an ad-hoc test. Conversely, if there are no notes for a given exploratory test, or if the notes are directed more at guiding the testing effort than at reproducing the test, then this is almost surely an ad-hoc test.

Comparison of Ad-hoc and Regression tests:

An Ad-hoc test can be described as an exploratory case that is expected to be run only once, unless it uncovers a defect.

Regression testing is the process of testing the modifications to the programs to ensure that the old program still works as it was, with the new changes. Regression testing is a normal part of the program development process and in larger companies is done by code reviewing/ testing specialists. Testing department coders develop code test scenarios and exercises that will test new units of code after they have been included. These test cases form what becomes the test bucket. For instance, before a new version of a software product is released, the old test cases are run against on the new version to make sure that all the old capabilities still hold. The reason they might not work is on account of changing or adding new code to a program can easily introduce errors into code that is not intended to be changed.

In particular, each method has strengths and weaknesses in the critical dimensions of defect finding power and confidence building. A primary goal of ad-hoc testing is to uncover new defects in the product. In the hands of a skilled tester, it can be highly effective at discovering such problems. As a confidence builder, ad-hoc testing is relatively weak, compared with formal regression testing, which can be a powerful confidence builder, especially if the breadth and depth of the coverage is demonstrably high.

Regression testing is the opposite of ad-hoc testing in the sense that, an implicit yet important attribute of a regression test is that it is expected to be re-run, in contrast to an ad-hoc test, which is expected to be run only once.

Although they are at the opposite ends of the spectrum, regression tests and ad-hoc tests complement each other in remarkable ways. Ironically, when the tester uncovers a defect with either form of testing, he will be drawn towards the opposite end of the spectrum. When he finds a defect with a regression test, he will often need to use ad-hoc methods to analyze and isolate the defect and to narrow down the steps to reproduce it. He may also want to "explore around" the defect to determine, if there are related problems. On the other hand, when he finds a defect with an ad-hoc test, he will probably document it in his defect tracking system, thereby turning it into a regression test, for verification after the defect is fixed.

Some other specific types of testing along this spectrum may also be considered. For the sake of easy visualization, fully repeatable regression tests are placed on the left end of the spectrum and ad-hoc tests on the right end. For any given method used by a tester, its location along this spectrum will vary, depending on the methods being used by the tester. For example, performance testing and release testing have a dominant regression testing component; hence they are placed along the left side of the spectrum. Exploratory testing and User Scenario testing have a dominant ad-hoc component, hence they are placed somewhere on the right side of the spectrum.

The Metaphorical Bridge:

The spectrum described above can also be pictured as a bridge between formal and less formal testing paradigms. This metaphor has the advantage of suggesting motion across the bridge in both directions. For example, regression tests can be brought across the bridge into the ad-hoc domain for more extensive testing. Conversely, ad-hoc tests that have to be re-run can be brought across the bridge in the other direction, for integration with the regression suite.

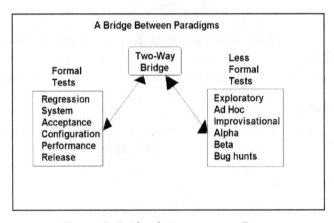

Figure 2: Bridge between paradigms

2.2.2 Improvisational Testing

One approach to ad-hoc testing is to treat it as improvisation on a theme. Testers start with a documented Test Design that systematically describes all the cases to be covered.

One of the more productive ways to perform improvisational testing is to gather a group of two or more skilled testers in the same room and ask them to collaborate on extemporaneous testing. The collaborators are provided with individual machines for testing. On the basis of anecdotal evidence, the defect finding power of people collaborating in this way is considerably greater than the sum of its parts, so there appears to be a high potential for group synergy with improvisational testing.

Another way to approach improvisational testing is by using existing documented tests as the initial theme and then inventing variations on that theme. For example, imagine that an image editing program named Panorama, which stitches together a series of photographs into a seamless panoramic image, is being tested.

The series of steps that would be required to carry out the test are:

1. Load the Panorama program
2. Import 8 photographic images that together represent a full 360 degree panorama
3. Invoke the auto-stitching feature
4. Verify that the auto-stitching sequence completes without errors
5. Verify that the resulting image is seamlessly stitched into a 360-degree vista
6. If any of the stitches are not aligned correctly, invoke the manual stitching feature
7. Manually align any stitches that look incorrect
8. Invoke the final stitch feature
9. Verify that the final stitch feature completes without errors
10. Verify that the resulting panorama looks correct.

The desired result is an aesthetically pleasing and perceptually convincing panoramic image, but there may be many different resulting images that would pass the test.

The 10 steps listed above contain a repeating pattern: 3 execution steps, then 2 verification steps, followed again by 3 execution steps and 2 verification steps. Testers often fall into patterns like this without even realizing it, which limits the types of tests they design. Therefore, one simple way to introduce a variation would be to alter that pattern. This could be done in any number of ways, such as inserting new steps into the test-case that would not alter the end result. For example:

- Step 3 (auto-stitching) could be run two or more times in succession before proceeding to step 4.
- Manually align the stitches first, prior to running the auto-stitch algorithm and then proceed as before
- Between any two steps, system's display color depth settings (the number of colors displayed) can be toggled back and forth before proceeding.

The possibilities are nearly endless.

The major advantages of improvisational testing are:

- Improvisational Testing is a craft. It is the desire to narrow the field to the cases that are most likely to uncover problems.
- Improvisational techniques are particularly useful when verifying that defects have been fixed. Rather than simply verifying that the steps to reproduce the defect no longer result in the error, the improvisational tester explores "around" the fix, inventing variations on the steps to reproduce the original defect, ensuring

more fully that the fix did not have undesirable side effects elsewhere.

This is explained using the above example. Let us say that a defect has been found such that when any of the stitches is adjusted manually, all the stitches to the left of the one adjusted become misaligned. After the defect is fixed, the seams to the left are now behaving properly. In addition to this, some additional tests can also be improvised, such as verifying that the stitches to the right of a manually aligned stitch still behave properly too.

Improvising in this way is an example of crossing the bridge from the formal towards the less formal testing methods.

Let us assume that from the currently existing documented test ten new variations are invented on that case through improvising. Of those ten, perhaps one of them uncovers a new defect, eight of them are run as one-off tests (those that are discarded after running them once) and one has been decided to be added to the regression suite. In the case of the two new tests that have to be re-run (the defect and the one added to the regression suite), a decision has to be made to carry them back across the metamorphic bridge in the other direction.

Some factors to be considered for this purpose are:

Assume the test is run once and that it has passed the test. Next, make an educated guess as to what the probability is that re-running this test in the future will uncover an important defect. Some factors to be considered to make this decision include:

- Does this feature reside in a relatively unstable area of the program?

- Can this test be automated easily, so that it can be re-run many times at lower execution cost?
- If this test was to fail, what would be the severity level of the defect?

One way in which improvisational tests differ from ordinary ad-hoc tests is with ad-hoc tests there is no expectation to re-run them unless a defect is found, but with improvisational tests, cases that would be appropriate to preserve are carefully looked for and re-run as part of regression suite. For this reason, Improvisational Testing is placed closer to the middle of the spectrum between regression and ad-hoc testing.

Strengths of Ad-hoc Testing:

One of the best uses of ad-hoc testing is for discovery. Reading the requirements or specifications rarely gives a good sense of how a program actually behaves. Even the user documentation may not capture the "look and feel" of a program. Ad-hoc testing can find holes in the test strategy and can expose relationships between sub-systems that would otherwise not be apparent. In this sense, it serves as a tool for checking the completeness of testing method. Missing cases can be found and added to the testing arsenal. Finding new tests in this way can also be a sign that root-cause analysis should be performed. Defects found while doing ad-hoc testing are often examples of entire classes of forgotten test cases.

Another use for ad-hoc testing is to determine the priorities for other testing activities. In our example, Panorama may allow the user to sort photographs that are being displayed. If ad-hoc testing shows this to work well, the formal testing of this feature might be deferred until the problematic areas are completed. On the other hand, if ad-hoc testing of this sorting photograph feature uncovers problems, then the formal testing might receive a higher priority.

Ad-hoc testing can also be used effectively to increase code coverage. Adding new tests to formal test designs often requires a lot of effort in producing the designs, implementing the tests and finally determining the improved coverage. A more streamlined approach involves using iterative ad-hoc tests to determine quickly whether code coverage is added.

There are two general classes of functions in the code that forms most programs - functions that support a specific feature and basic low-level housekeeping functions. It is for these housekeeping functions that ad-hoc testing is particularly valuable, because many of these functions would not make it into the specifications or user documentation. The testing team may well be unaware of the code's existence.

2.3 Conclusion

Software testing is a critical element in SDLC and has the potential to save time and money by identifying problems early and to improve customer satisfaction by delivering a more defect-free product. Unfortunately, it is often less formal and rigorous than it should and a primary reason for that is because the project staff is unfamiliar with software testing methodologies, approaches and tools. Without adequate testing, however, there is a greater risk that an application will inadequately deliver what was expected by the business users or that the final product will have problems such that users will eventually abandon it out of frustration. In either case, time and money are lost and the credibility and reputation of the developers is damaged. More formal, rigorous testing will go far to reducing the risk that these scenarios occur. The testing type to be chosen has to be a blend of all types of tests. A single test cannot fulfill the testing requirement efficiently. It has to be a blend of all type of tests. The type of test purely depends on the test case while there are certain factors to be considered which can be applied to most of the test cases which are listed in the improvisation test.

*****

Chapter 3 - Design of Experiments – An Overview

Design of Experiments (DoE) is a systematic approach to investigation of a system or process. A series of structured tests are designed in which planned changes are made to the input variables of a process or system. The effects of these changes on a pre-defined output are then assessed.

Design of Experiment (DoE) can also be defined as a structured, organized method that is used to determine the relationship between the different factors (Xs) affecting a process and the output of that process (Ys). This method was first developed in the 1920s and 1930, by **Sir Ronald A. Fisher,** the renowned Mathematician and Geneticist.

The word **design** in the phrase **design of experiments** refers to the way in which variables are intentionally varied over many runs in an experiment. Once the experimental variables are identified and the levels of each variable are chosen, the experiment can be designed. Usually the experiment design is expressed in the form of two matrices: a **variable matrix** and a **design matrix**.

DoE is important as a formal way of maximizing information gained while minimizing resources required. It has more to offer than "one change at a time" experimental methods; because it allows a judgment on the significance to the output of input variables acting alone, as well input variables acting in combination with one another.

"One change at a time" testing always carries the risk that the experimenter may find one input variable to have a significant effect on the response (output) while failing to discover that changing another variable may alter the effect of the first (i.e. some kind of dependency or interaction). This is because the temptation is to stop the test when this first significant effect has been found. In order to reveal an interaction or dependency, "one change at a time" testing relies on the experimenter carrying the tests in the appropriate direction. However, DoE plans for all possible dependencies in the first place and then prescribes exactly what data are needed to assess them i.e. whether input variables change the response on their own, when combined, or not at all. In terms of resource the exact length and size of the experiment are set by the design (i.e. before testing begins).

When to use DoE?

DoE can be used to find answers in situations such as:

- What is the main contributing factor to a problem?
- How well does the system/ process perform in the presence of noise?
- What is the best configuration of factor values to minimize variation in a response?
- Etc.

In general, these questions are given labels as particular types of study. In the examples discussed earlier, these are problem solving, parameter design and robustness study. In each case, DoE is used to find the answer; the only thing that marks them different is which factors would be used in the experiment.

Basic Concepts: Any process can simply be explained as:

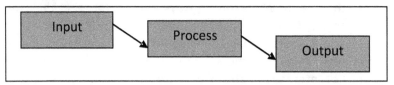

Figure 3: A simple process

Processes have inputs that determine how the process operates and outputs that are produced by the process. Experiments/ Tests are performed to document the behavior of the outputs corresponding to various inputs for scientific purposes, but the goal of engineering experimentation is to learn how to control the process inputs in order to produce the desired outputs.

Process inputs are called **variables, factors or predictors** and process outputs are called **responses**.

Every experiment involves the observation of both the inputs (the variables) and the outputs (the responses). The action taken by the tester on the inputs determines whether the experiment is passive or active. When the experimenter merely observes the system and records any changes that occur in the inputs and the corresponding outputs, the experiment is **passive**. This type of experimentation can be costly, time-consuming and unproductive. When the experimenter intentionally varies the inputs, then the experiment is **active**. Active experimentation, done under controlled conditions in a logical structured manner, is the type of experimentation used in DoE.

3.1 Types of variables

Variables can be classified as:

➢ Intentionally varied
➢ Fixed
➢ Uncontrolled
  ○ Measurable
  ○ Non measurable

The relationship between the levels of a variable determines whether the variable is qualitative or quantitative.

The management of interaction between variables is the strength of DoE and a weakness of OVAT.

DoE recognizes and quantifies variable interactions so that they can be used to understand and better manage the response.

3.2 Types of responses

Whenever possible the response of an experiment should be quantitative. Any appropriate measurement system may be used, but it should be repeatable and reproducible. The responses are also referred to as levels. The different levels a variable can take is a major factor in the study of design of experiments.

The responses can majorly be classified as:

➢ Quantitative – marks in a given range
➢ Binary – passed or not (the factor here is the result and the level is 2- passed not passed)
➢ Qualitative – tasty, good, etc.

3.3   Identification of Variables and Responses

The best way to identify and document the many variables and responses of a process is to construct a cause-and-effect diagram. Let us consider the example shown in the below figure. The problem of interest is the performance of a two-part epoxy used Inputs Outputs.

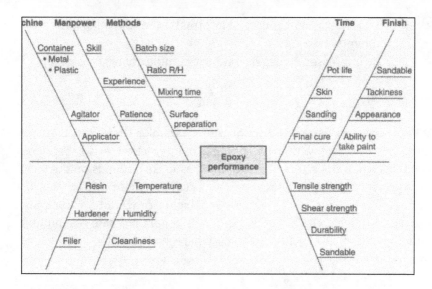

Figure 4: Cause-and-effect diagram

The process inputs are shown on the left and the responses are shown on the right. It can be noted that this diagram is just an elaboration of the simple process model in the earlier figure. It is very important to keep a cause-and-effect diagram for an experiment. Also the cause-and-effect diagram should be updated religiously as new variables and responses are identified.

The cause-and-effect diagram:

- Also called as Fish-bone diagram (since it is in that shape) or Epoxy diagram
- Provides a convenient place to collect ideas for new variables.
- Serves as a quick reference tool when things go wrong and quick decisions are necessary.
- Summarizes all of the variable considerations made over the life of the experiment.

- Provides an excellent source of information for planning new experiments.
- Quickly impresses managers with the complexity of the problem.

Interactions:

When a process contains two or more variables, it is possible that some will interact with each other. An interaction exists between variables when the effect of one on the response depends on the level of another variable. Interactions can occur between two, three, or more variables but three-variable and higher-order interactions are usually assumed to be insignificant. This is generally a safe assumption although there are certain systems where higher-order interactions are important.

With practice, two-factor interactions between variables can often be identified by simple graphs of the experimental response plotted as a function of the two involved variables. These plots usually show the response plotted as a function of one of the variables with the levels of the other variable distinguished by different types of lines or symbols. Multi-van charts are also useful for identifying variable interactions.

The management of interactions between variables is one of the strengths of the DoE method and a weakness of the one-variable-at-a-time (OVAT) method. Whereas DoE recognizes and quantifies variable interactions so that they can be used to understand and better manage the response, the OVAT method ignores the interactions and hence it will fail in certain cases when the effects of those interactions are relatively large. DoE's success comes from its consideration of all possible combinations of variable levels. OVAT fails because it relies on a simple but flawed algorithm to determine how the variables affect the response. In some cases, OVAT will obtain the same result as DoE, but in many other cases its result will be inferior.

3.4   Selection of Variable Levels

The selection of the variable levels for a designed experiment is a very serious issue. Many experiments fail because the levels of one or more variables are chosen incorrectly. Even when a variable level is chosen badly and much of data are lost; the DoE method can often recover lots of information from the surviving data. This is one aspect of the robustness provided by DoE.

Qualitative Variables: For qualitative variables the choice of levels is not so critical. Just to be ensured that each level is practical and should give valid data. Always it has to be tried to redefine a qualitative variable to make it quantitative. Even if it is not chosen to analyze or interpret it in this way, it provides increased understanding of how the variable behaves.

Sometimes qualitative variables can have only two levels: yes or no – i.e. binary. Many process variables behave like this— either the step is done in the process or not. For example, if surface preparation for epoxy is done by sanding, then the surface might be sanded or not sanded.

Quantitative Variables: The selection of levels for quantitative variables can become quite complicated. The most important issue is the choice of the highest and lowest levels. These levels must be safe, that is, the product obtained at these levels should be useful or at least the process should be able to operate at these levels. This tends to force the choice of levels to be narrow so there's less risk of losing runs or doing damage. If, however, the levels are chosen too close together, no difference may be seen between them and something important outside of the range of experimentation may be missed. Experimenters are always trying to guess the highest and lowest safe levels for variables so that they have a high likelihood of seeing measurable effects on the responses. This is often a difficult and nerve-wracking task and it is very important to include the experts, operators and managers who are knowledgeable of and responsible for the process because they are the ones most likely to offer valuable guidance.

To emphasize the importance of picking the highest and lowest levels of quantitative variables in an experiment, suppose that there are five variables in an experiment. If the safe range of operation for each variable is known, but only one half of that range is used just to be really safe, then the five-variable experiment will only cover $(1/2) = 0.031$ or three percent of the possible design space. The chances of finding a good design are significantly reduced by using too narrow a range for the variables. This is a very common mistake made by novice experimenters.

When three or more levels of a quantitative variable are used in an experiment, there are several ways to choose the spacing between levels. The most common choice for a three-level quantitative variable is to use three equally spaced levels, often denoted with the coded values -1, 0 and $+1$ or just $-$, 0 and $+$. For example, if the batch-size variable in uses three levels of 50, 100 and 150cc, then the levels are referred to using the codes -1, 0 and $+1$, respectively.

When the increment between levels is constant, we say that we have a linear scale for that variable. It is also possible to design level selections using other schemes. For example, levels can be selected on the basis of squares (for example, 1, 4, 9) or on a log scale (for example, 3, 6, 12). In each case, the three levels are still referenced with the codes -1, 0 and $+1$. The use of special scaling for levels is usually based on the experimenter's understanding of the response and its expected dependence on the study variable.

NESTED VARIABLES: Sometimes it is impossible or impractical for the levels of one variable to be expressed within each level of another variable. In this case we say that one variable is **nested** within another. For instance, let us consider a manufacturing process in which two machines (x1: A or B) are supposed to be producing the same material and that each machine has eight heads or stations (x2: 1 to 8) that are all supposed to perform the exactly the same operation. (Since the product that flows into these two machines gets separated into 16 separate but hopefully identical channels, this is called a multiple stream process.) It is not logical to try to compare pairs of heads with other pairs of heads, such as the two heads with x2 = 1 on machines A and B with the two heads x2 = 2, since they are physically different heads. The comparison is just not meaningful. Instead, we say that heads are nested within machines and treat each head as the unique one that it is. In order to un-nest the heads it would be necessary to redefine the head variable as having 16 levels (x2: 1 to 16) and physically move the heads to each of the 16 different positions on the two machines.

Another example of nesting is when two manufacturers (x1: A or B) are each asked to provide three different lots of material for evaluation. Someone might choose to identify each manufacturer's lots with identification numbers 1, 2 and 3 (x2: 1, 2, 3), but lot 1 from manufacturer A has no relationship to lot 1 from manufacturer B other than that they have the same identification number. It would be just as appropriate and perhaps clearer, to identify the lots as 1, 2 and 3 for manufacturer A and 4, 5 and 6 for manufacturer B. Regardless of how the lots are numbered, they are nested within manufacturers.

COVARIATES: An uncontrolled quantitative variable that can be measured during the experiment is called a covariate. Common covariates are variables like temperature, atmospheric pressure, humidity and line voltage. If the covariate has no influence on the response, then it is of no consequence, but in most cases it is unclear whether the covariate is important or not. All known variables that are uncontrolled during the experiment are covariates and should be measured and recorded. Then when the statistical analysis of the experimental data is performed, the effect of these covariates can be removed from the response. Generally, the effect of the covariate should have a very small if not immeasurable effect on the response. If the effect of a covariate becomes too large, it can interfere with estimates of the effects of other variables.

Covariates must be continuous (that is, quantitative) variables. They are always analyzed using regression methods. For this reason, the word *covariate* is also used to refer to quantitative variables that are intentionally varied in the experiment, even if they only appear at two discrete levels, because they are also analyzed with regression methods.

3.5 Replication and Repetition

The design matrix of an experiment determines what terms the model will be capable of resolving, but the sensitivity of the analysis to small variable effects is determined by the number of times each experimental run is built. Generally, the more times the runs of an experiment design are built the greater will be the sensitivity of the experiment.

There are two different ways that the runs of an experiment design can be repeated. When consecutive units are made without changing the levels of the design variables between units, these like units are called **repetitions**. When two or more like units are produced in an experiment, but at different times spaced throughout the experiment and not as consecutive units, these like units are called **replicates.**

DoE novices usually have difficulty using and understanding the word replicate because it is used as both a noun and a verb and is even pronounced differently in the two cases. As a noun, the word replicate is used to refer to each set of unique runs that make up a complete experiment design. As a verb, it replicates an experiment design by building replicates.

At first it might seem that the use of repetitions and replicates would give similar, if not identical, results but that is usually not the case. Indeed, the values of the response for both repetitions and replicates will be nearly identical if the process is stable, but replication almost always leads to greater variation in the response due to changes in uncontrolled variables. Despite this apparent disadvantage of replication over repetition, replication generally provides a more realistic measure of the inherent noise in the process and is the preferred way to increase the number of runs in an experiment. The difference in the values associated with repetitions and replicates is made clear by how they are treated in statistical analyses; repeated runs are averaged whereas individual replicated observations are preserved, hence repetitions do comparatively little to increase the sensitivity of an experiment to small variable effects.

The number of replicates required for an experiment is often chosen arbitrarily, based on historical choices or guidelines, but should instead be determined by an objective sample-size calculation. The inputs required to complete such sample size calculations are:

1. An estimate of the inherent error variation in the process,

2. The size of the smallest variable effect considered to be practically significant

3. Knowledge of the model to be fitted to the experimental data. When one or more of these values are unknown, they should be estimated by considering prior experience with similar processes, information from preliminary experiments, or expert opinion.

It is very important that the number of replicates per cell in the experiment design be held constant. An unequal number of replicates throws off the balance of the experiment and can lead to biased or even incorrect conclusions. The balance of the experiment is referred to as its **orthogonality** and it is said that an unbalanced experiment has suffered some loss of orthogonality. There is a rigorous mathematical meaning to the term orthogonality, but still only used in a binary sense to address the issue of whether the experiment is balanced or not. Often an experiment intended to have an equal number of replicates suffers from some loss of units due to breakage or early product failure. Some experiments, especially those that are replicated several times, can tolerate lost units, but recovering the integrity of an experiment with a substantial loss of orthogonality requires finesse and experience. Some recommendations on how to deal with a few lost units will be presented in this book, but plan on replacing lost units if it is at all possible and consult with the neighborhood statistician when it is not. Some experiments can be fractionally replicated. Fractionally replicated experiments use only certain runs, such as one half or one quarter of all of the possible runs. If they are carefully designed, these experiments can be very efficient but they do have limitations, such as the inherent confounding (or aliasing) of variables and interactions. If the confounding is managed correctly, a fractionally replicated experiment can provide most of the information that a fully replicated experiment would reveal.

The randomization of replicates can take two forms: complete randomization and limited randomization. In complete randomization, all runs of all replicates are eligible to be run at any time. With limited randomization, all of the runs of each replicate are completed before the next replicate is started, with the runs within each replicate performed in random order. This approach, called **blocking on replicates**, has the advantage that biases between the blocked replicates, that would otherwise be attributed to experimental noise, can be isolated in the experiment analysis. By isolating the block biases the experimental error is reduced which increases the sensitivity of the experiment to small variable effects. This advantage makes blocking on replicates the preferred practice over complete randomization.

3.6 Effect of Signal to Noise Ratio

The more times a given set of conditions is replicated, the more precisely the response can be estimated. Replication improves the chance of detecting a statistically significant effect (the signal) in the midst of natural process variation (the noise). In some processes, the noise drowns out the signal. Before a Design of Experiment (DoE) is started, it helps to assess the signal-to-noise ratio. Then number of runs that will be required for the DoE can be found out. First how much of a signal that can be detected has to be found out. Then the noise can be estimated. This can be determined from control charts, process capability studies, analysis of variance (ANOVA) from prior DoEs or a best guess based on experience.

Based on the number of times to replicate a given set of conditions, the response can be estimated precisely. Replication improves the chance of detecting a statistically significant effect (the signal) in the midst of natural process variation (the noise).

Table **3:** Number of runs as a function of signal to noise ratio

Signal-to-Noise Ratio(Δ/σ)	Minimum Number of Runs
1.0	64
1.4	32
2.0	16
2.8	8

The statisticians who developed two-level factorial designs incorporated 'hidden' replication within the test matrices. The level of replication is a direct function of the size of the DoE. The data in the table can be used to determine the number of runs required in two-level factorial runs in order to provide a 90-percent probability of detecting the desired signal. If it cannot be afford to do the necessary runs, then alternates to decrease the noise has to be looked out. For instance, above table shows a minimum of 64 runs for a signal-to-noise ratio of 1. However, if the noise could not be cut to half, the signal-to-noise ratio would double (to 2), thus reducing the runs from 64 to 16. If the noise cannot be reduced, then it must be accepted an increase in the detectable signal (the minimum effect that will be revealed by the DoE).

The power of DoE can be improved by adding actual replicates where conditions are duplicated. It cannot be just got by with repeat samples or measurements. The entire process must be repeated from start to finish. If several samples are submitted from a given experimental run, the response will be average.

Consider the case of injection molding; control charts reveal a standard deviation of 0.60. Management wants to detect an effect of magnitude 0.85. Therefore, the signal-to-noise ratio is approximately 1.4. The appropriate number of runs for this two-level factorial experiment is 32. We decide not to add further replicates due to time constraints, but several parts will be made from each run. The response for each run becomes the average shrinkage per part, thus dampening out variability in parts and the measurement itself.

*****

Chapter 4 - Experimental Design

An **Experimental Design** is the laying out of a detailed experimental plan in advance of doing the experiment. Well-chosen experimental designs maximize the amount of 'information' that can be obtained for a given amount of experimental effort.

The statistical theory underlying DoE generally begins with the concept of **process models**.

4.1 Process Model

The word **model** refers to the mathematical description of how the response behaves as a function of the input variable or variables. A good model explains the systematic behavior of the original data in some concise manner. The specific form of the model depends on the type of design variable used in the experiment. If an experiment contains a single qualitative design variable set to several different treatment levels, then the model consists of the treatment means. There will be as many means for the model as there are treatments in the experiment. If an experiment contains a single quantitative variable that covers a range of values, then the model will consist of an equation that relates the response to the quantitative predictor.

Experiments that involve qualitative predictors are usually analyzed by analysis of variance (ANOVA) method.

Experiments that involve quantitative predictors are usually analyzed by **regression** method.

Experiments that combine both qualitative and quantitative variables are analyzed using a special regression model called a **general linear model**.

Black box process model: It is common to begin with a process model of the 'black box' type, with several discrete or continuous input factors that can be controlled--that is, varied at will by the experimenter--and one or more measured output responses. The output responses are assumed continuous. Experimental data are used to derive an empirical (approximation) model linking the outputs and inputs. These empirical models generally contain first (linear) and second-order terms (quadratic).

Often the experiment has to account for a number of uncontrolled factors that may be discrete, such as different machines or operators, and/or continuous such as ambient temperature or humidity. The below figure illustrates this situation – it is a Schematic diagram of a typical process with controlled inputs, outputs, discrete uncontrolled factors and continuous uncontrolled factors.

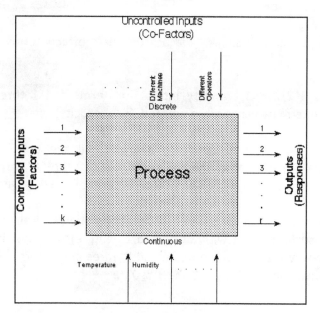

Figure 5: Schematic diagram

Linear model: A linear model with two factors, X_1 and X_2, can be written as:

$Y = \beta_0 + \beta_1 X_1 + \beta_2 X_2 + \beta_{12} X_1 X_2 +$ experimental error

Here, Y is the response for given levels of the main effects X_1 and X_2. The $X_1 X_2$ term is included to account for a possible interaction effect between X_1 and X_2. The constant β_0 is the response of Y when both main effects are 0.

For a more complicated example, a linear model with three factors X_1, X_2, X_3 and one response, Y, would look like (if all possible terms were included in the model)

$Y = \beta_0 + \beta_1 X_1 + \beta_2 X_2 + \beta_3 X_3 + \beta_{12} X_1 X_2 + \beta_{13} X_1 X_3 + \beta_{23} X_2 X_3 + \beta_{123} X_1 X_2 X_3 +$ experimental error

The three terms with single "X's" are the **main effects** terms. There are:

$k(k-1)/2 = 3*2/2 = 3$ **two-way interaction** terms and 1 **three-way** interaction term (which is often omitted, for simplicity).

When the experimental data are analyzed, all the unknown 'β' parameters are estimated and the coefficients of the "X" terms are tested to see which ones are significantly different from 0.

Quadratic model: A second-order (quadratic) model (typically used in **response surface** DoE's with suspected curvature) does not include the three-way interaction term but adds three more terms to the linear model, namely $\beta_{11} X_1^2 + \beta_{22} X_2^2 + \beta_{33} X_3^2$.

Each model should definitely contain a certain variable for accommodating error during experimentation. Depending upon the different conditions of measurement the type of analysis is chosen.

4.2 Types of Design

Two of the primary considerations that distinguish experiment designs are the number of design variables that they include and the complexity of the model that they provide. For a specified number of design variables, there could be many experiment designs to choose from, but the extreme designs that span all of the others are called screening experiments and response surface experiments. The major types of design are:

4.2.1 Comparative designs

Primarily Comparative designs are of two types:

- To choose between alternatives, with narrow scope, suitable for an initial comparison
- To choose between alternatives, with broad scope, suitable for a confirmatory comparison

Screening designs are used to study a large number of design variables for the purpose of identifying the most important ones. Some screening experiments can evaluate many variables with a very few experimental runs. Screening experiments use only two levels of each design variable and cannot resolve interactions between pairs of variables — a characteristic which can make these designs quite risky.

Response Surface modeling is to achieve one or more of the following objectives:

- Hit a target
- Maximize or minimize a response
- Reduce variation by locating a region where the process is easier to manage
- Make a process robust

Response-surface experiments are more complex and difficult to administrate than screening experiments, hence they generally involve just two to five variables. Every variable in a response surface design must be quantitative and three or more levels of each variable will be required. The benefit of using so many variable levels is that response surface designs provide very complex models that include at least main effects, two- factor interactions and terms to measure the curvature induced in the response by each design variable.

There is an intermediate set of experiment designs that falls between screening experiments and response surface experiments in terms of their complexity and capability. These experiments typically use two levels of each design variable and can resolve main effects, two-factor interactions and sometimes higher-order interactions. When the design variables are all quantitative, a select set of additional runs with intermediate variable levels can be included in these designs to provide a test for, but not complete resolution of, curvature in the response. The existence of this family of intermediate designs should make it apparent that there is actually a discrete spectrum of experiment designs for a given number of experimental variables, where the spectrum is bounded by screening and response surface designs.

4.3 Regression modeling

Regression modeling is - to estimate a precise model, quantifying the dependence of response variable(s) on process inputs.

When faced with a new situation where there is little prior knowledge or experience, the best strategy may be to employ a series of smaller experiments instead of committing all available time and resources to one large experiment. The first experiment that should be considered is a screening experiment to determine the most influential variables from among the many variables that could affect the process. A screening experiment for many variables will usually identify the two or three significant variables that dominate the process. The next step in the series of experiments would be to build a more complex experiment involving the key variables identified by the screening experiment. This design should at least be capable of resolving two-factor interactions, but often the chosen design is a response surface design which can more completely characterize the process being studied. Occasionally when such a series of experiments is planned, the insights provided by the early experiments are sufficient to indicate an effective solution to the problem that initiated the project, victory can be declared and the experimental program can be suspended.

Usually the experiment design is expressed in the form of two matrices: a **variable matrix** and a **design matrix**.

The purpose of the Variable Matrix is to clearly define the experimental variables and their levels.

4.4 Key steps of DoE

Obtaining good results from a DoE involves these seven steps:

1. Set objectives
2. Select process variables
3. Select an experimental design
4. Execute the design

5. Check that the data are consistent with the experimental assumptions
6. Analyze and interpret the results
7. Use or present the results (may lead to further runs or DoE's).

4.4.1 Objectives

Planning an experiment begins with careful consideration of what the objectives (or goals) are; the objectives for an experiment are best determined by a team discussion.

The group should discuss which objectives are the key ones and which ones are "nice but not really necessary". Prioritization of the objectives helps to decide which direction to go with regard to the selection of the factors, responses and the particular design. Sometimes prioritization will force to start over from scratch when it will be realized that the experiment decided earlier to be run does not meet one or more critical objectives.

4.4.2 Selection of Process Variables

Process variables include both **inputs** and **outputs** - i.e., **factors** and **responses**. The selection of these variables is best done as a team effort.

The team should consist of:

* Include all important factors.
* Choose the low and high factor levels.
* Check the factor settings for impractical or impossible combinations
* Include all relevant responses.

- Avoid using only responses that combine two or more measurements of the process.

When the range of the settings for input factors are chosen, it is wise to give some thought beforehand rather than just try extreme values. In some cases, extreme values will give runs that are not feasible; in other cases, extreme ranges might move one out of a smooth area of the response surface into some jagged region, or close to an asymptote. **Two-level designs** have just a **high** and a **low** setting for each factor. The most popular experimental designs are two-level designs. The main reason for choosing two levels is that it is ideal for screening designs, simple and economical; it also gives most of the information required to go to a multilevel response surface experiment if one is needed. Consider adding some center points to the two-level design. The term "two-level design" is something of a misnomer, however, as it is recommended to include some center points during the experiment.

Matrix notation for describing an experiment: The standard layout for a 2-level design uses +1 and -1 notation to denote the "high level" and the "low level" respectively, for each factor. For example, the matrix below describes an experiment in which 4 trials (or runs) were conducted with each factor set to high or low during a run according to whether the matrix had a +1 or -1 set for the factor during that trial. If the experiment had more than 2 factors, there would be an additional column in the matrix for each additional factor.

Table **4**: Matrix notation for describing an experiment

	Factor 1 (X1)	Factor 2 (X2)
Trial 1	-1	-1
Trial 2	+1	-1
Trial 3	-1	+1
Trial 4	+1	+1

4.4.3   Coding the data

The use of +1 and -1 for the factor settings is called **coding** the data. This aids in the interpretation of the coefficients fit to any experimental model. After factor settings are coded, center points have the value '0'.

The Model or Analysis Matrix (design matrices):

If we add an 'I' column and an "X1 * X2" column to the matrix of 4 trials for a two-factor experiment described earlier, we obtain what is known as the **model or analysis matrix** for this simple experiment, which is shown below.

Table **5:** Design Matrices

I	X1	X2	X1 * X2
+1	-1	-1	+1
+1	+1	-1	-1
+1	-1	+1	-1
+1	+1	+1	+1

Model for the experiment: The model for this experiment is:

$$Y = \beta_0 + \beta_1 X_1 + \beta_2 X_2 + \beta_{12} X_1 X_2 + \text{experimental error}$$

and the 'I' column of the design matrix has all 1's to provide for the β_0 term. The X1 * X2 column is formed by multiplying the 'X1' and 'X2' columns together, row element by row element. This column gives interaction term for each trial.

Model in matrix notation: In matrix notation, we can summarize this experiment by

$Y = X * \beta$ + experimental error

for which X is the 4 by 4 design matrix of 1's and -1's shown above, β is the vector of unknown model coefficients (β_0, β_1, β_2, β_{12}) and Y is a vector consisting of the four trial response observations.

4.4.4   Selection of Experimental Design

A design is selected based on the experimental objective and the number of factors: The choice of an experimental design depends on the objectives of the experiment and the number of factors to be investigated.

Orthogonal Property of Scaling in a 2-Factor Experiment – Coding produces orthogonal columns. Coding is sometime called **orthogonal coding** since all the columns of a coded 2-factor design matrix (except the 'I' column) are typically orthogonal i.e. the dot product for any pair of columns is zero.

For example, for X1 and X2: (-1)(-1) + (+1)(-1) + (-1)(+1) + (+1)(+1) = 0.

Experimental Design Objectives: Various types of designs are listed according to the experimental objective they meet.

Comparative objective: If there are one or several factors under investigation, but the primary goal of the experiment is to make a conclusion about one a-priori important factor, (in the presence of, and/ or in spite of the existence of the other factors) and the question of interest is whether or not that factor is 'significant', (i.e., whether or not there is a significant change in the response for different levels of that factor), then it is a **comparative problem** and a **comparative design** solution is required.

Screening objective: The primary purpose of the experiment is to select or **screen out** the few important main effects from the many less important ones. These **screening designs** are also termed main effects designs.

Response Surface (method) objective: The experiment is designed to allow us to estimate interaction and even quadratic effects and therefore give us an idea of the (local) shape of the response surface we are investigating. For this reason, they are termed **response surface method (RSM) designs**. RSM designs are used to:

- Find improved or optimal process settings
- Troubleshoot process problems and weak points
- Make a product or process more *robust* against external and non-controllable influences. 'Robust' means relatively insensitive to these influences.

Optimizing responses when factors are proportions of a mixture objective: If there are factors that are proportions of a mixture and the requirement is to know what the 'best' proportions of the factors are so as to maximize (or minimize) a response, then need a **mixture design** is required.

Optimal fitting of a regression model objective: If the requirement is to model a response as a mathematical function (either known or empirical) of a few continuous factors and a 'good' model parameter estimates (i.e., unbiased and minimum variance) are desired, then a **regression design** is needed.

Table **6**: Comparative, screening & response surface designs

Design Selection Guideline			
Number of Factors	**Comparative Objective**	**Screening Objective**	**Response Surface Objective**
1	1-factor completely randomized design	-	-
2 – 4	Randomized block design	Full or fractional factorial	Central composite or Box-Behnken
5 or more	Randomized block design	Fractional factorial or Plackett-Burman	Screen first to reduce number of factors

There are different kinds of experimental designs. Generally they can be classified into large groups with strange names: factorials, 2 factorials, fractional factorials, central composite, Box-Behnken and Plackett-Burman. There are also hybrid designs which combine characteristics from two or more of these groups. Even though they may sound complicated only a handful of designs are used for the majority of experiments.

Resources and degree of control over wrong decisions: Choice of a design from within these various types depends on the amount of resources available and the degree of control over making wrong decisions that the experimenter desires.

Save some runs for center points and 'redo' that might be needed: It is a good idea to choose a design that requires somewhat fewer runs than the budget permits, so that center point runs can be added to check for curvature in a 2-level screening design and backup resources are available to redo runs that have processing.

4.4.5 Different types of Experimental Designs

Many an experimental design like Completely Randomized, Full Factorial, Partial Factorial, etc., is in vogue. Let us see some of them.

4.4.5.1 Completely Randomized Design

These designs are for studying the effects of one primary factor without the need to take other nuisance factors into account. Here we consider completely randomized designs that have one primary factor. The experiment compares the values of a response variable based on the different levels of that primary factor.

For completely randomized designs, the levels of the primary factor are randomly assigned to the experimental units. By randomization, we mean that the run sequence of the experimental units is determined randomly. For example, if there are 3 levels of the primary factor with each level to be run 2 times, then there are 6 factorial possible run sequences (or 6! ways to order the experimental trials). Because of the replication, the number of unique orderings is 90 [since 90 = 6!/(2! * 2! * 2!)]. An example of an un-randomized design would be to always run 2 replications for the first level, then 2 for the second level and finally 2 for the third level. To randomize the runs, one way would be to put 6 slips of paper in a box with 2 having level 1, 2 having level 2 and 2 having level 3. Before each run, one of the slips would be drawn blindly from the box and the level selected would be used for the next run of the experiment.

It is usually impossible to construct all of the runs of an experiment simultaneously, so runs are typically made one after the other. Since uncontrolled experimental conditions could change from run to run, the influence of the order of the runs must be considered.

Even a simple experiment with one variable at two levels would be easiest to build if all of its runs were done in a convenient order (for example, 11112222); however, such run order plans run the risk of mistakenly attributing the effect of an unobserved variable that changes during the experiment to the experimental variable. The accepted method of protecting against this risk is to randomize the run order of the levels of the experimental variable (for example, 21121221).

By randomizing, the effects of any unobserved systematic changes in the process unrelated to the experimental variable are uniformly and randomly distributed over all of the levels of the experimental variable. This inflates the error variability observed within experimental treatments, but it does not add bias to the real and interesting differences between treatments. An experiment with a single classification variable with several levels that are run in random order is called a **completely randomized design**.

Sometimes a variable must be included in an experiment even though it is not required in detecting or making claims about differences between its levels. For example, an experiment to compare several operators might require so many parts, that raw material for the parts must come from several different raw material lots. If the lot-to-lot differences are not important, then the experiment could be run using one lot at a time, one after the other. To be able to make valid claims about differences between operators, each operator would have to make parts using material from each lot and the operator order would have to be randomized within lots. For example, if there were four operators and three material lots, the following run order plan might be considered.

In this experiment, called a **randomized block design**, the raw material lots define blocks of runs and operator is the study variable. Because the blocks (that is, the raw material lots) are not run in random order, it is not safe to interpret any observed differences between them because the differences could be due to unobserved variables that change during the experiment. Since the operators are run in random order, it is safe to interpret differences between them as being real differences between operators. Even though the randomized block design has two variables, it is considered to be a one-variable experiment because claims can be made about only one of the two variables—always the study variable, which *must* be run in random order. Despite the loss of information about differences between the levels of the blocking variable, the use of blocking often increases the sensitivity of the experiment to differences between the levels of the study variable.

To summarize:

- If it is intended to make claims about differences between the treatment levels of a variable, then the run order of the treatment levels must be randomized.
- If a variable must be included in an experiment but it is not intended to make claims about differences between its levels, then the levels do not need to be randomized. Instead, the levels of the variable are used to define blocks of experimental runs.

Table **7**: Run Orders

Run Order	1	2	3	4	5	6	7	8	9	10	11.	12
Lot	A	A	A	A	B	B	B	B	C	C	C	C
Operator	2	1	3	4	4	3	2	1	2	4	3	1

Randomization typically performed by computer software: In practice, the randomization is typically performed by a computer program. However, the randomization can also be generated from random number tables or by some physical mechanism (e.g., drawing the slips of paper).

Three key numbers: All completely randomized designs with one primary factor are defined by 3 numbers:

k = number of factors (= 1 for these designs)
L = number of levels
n = number of replications

and the total sample size (number of runs) is $N = k * L * n$.

Balance: Balance dictates that the number of replications be the same at each level of the factor (this will maximize the sensitivity of subsequent statistical t {or F} tests).

Example of a completely randomized design A typical example of a completely randomized design is the following:

k = 1 factor ($X1$)
L = 4 levels of that single factor (called "1", "2", "3" and "4")
n = 3 replications per level
N = 4 levels * 3 replications per level = 12 runs

A sample randomized sequence of trials: The randomized sequence of trials might look like:

X1	4	2	1	3	4	3	2	3	1	4	3	1

It can be noted that in this example there are

$$12! / (3! * 3! * 3! * 3!) = 369,600$$

ways to run the experiment, all equally likely to be picked by a randomization procedure.

Model for a completely randomized design: The model for the response is

$$Y_{i,j} = \mu + T_i + \text{random error}$$

with

$Y_{i,j}$ being any observation for which $X1 = i$
 (i and j denote the level of the factor and the replication within the level of the factor, respectively)
μ (or mu) is the general location parameter
T_i is the effect of having treatment level i

Example

Contamination introduced during a powder dry process forms insoluble particles in the dried powder. A powder drying process introduces contamination that forms insoluble particles into the powder. When the powder is dissolved, these particles eventually clog a critical filter. An alternative drying schedule is proposed that should reduce the amount of contamination. Describe a run order plan for an experiment to compare the amount of insoluble particles formed in the two processes. A sample-size calculation based on historical process information indicates that 10 observations will be required from each drying process.

Solution: The simplest way to run the experiment would be to configure the drying system for the first process and then to complete all 10 trials before reconfiguring the system for the second process and its 10 trials. The run order would be 11111111112222222222. However, due to possible changes in raw material, temperature, humidity, concentration of the contaminant, the measurement process and so on, during the experiment, the 20 experimental trials should be performed in random order, such as: 22122121211122111212. Then if one or more unobserved variables do change and have an effect on the response, these effects will be randomly but uniformly applied to both treatments and not affect the true difference between the treatments.

4.4.5.2 Full Factorial Designs

A full factorial design of experiment (DoE) measures the response of every possible combination of factors and factor levels. These responses are analyzed to provide information about every main effect and every interaction effect. A full factorial DoE is practical when fewer than five factors are being investigated. Testing all combinations of factor levels becomes too expensive and time-consuming with five or more factors.

A frequently used factorial experiment design in the DoE is known as the **2^k factorial design or Two level Factorial design**, which is basically an experiment involving k factors, each of which has two levels ('low' and 'high'). In such a multi-factor two-level experiment, the number of treatment combinations needed to get complete results is equal to 2^k. Thus, a 2^k factorial experiment that deals with 3 factors would require 8 treatment combination, while one that deals with 4 factors would require 16 of them.

Table 8: Full Factorial Design

Number of Runs for a 2^k Full Factorial	
Number of Factors	**Number of Runs**
2	4
3	8
4	16
5	32
6	64
7	128

The first objective of a factorial experiment is to be able to determine, or at least estimate, the factor effects, which indicate how each factor affects the process output. Factor effects need to be understood so that the factors can be adjusted to optimize the process output.

The effect of each factor on the output can be due to it alone (a main effect of the factor), or a result of the interaction between the factor and one or more of the other factors (interactive effects). When assessing factor effects (whether main or interactive effects), one needs to consider not only the magnitudes of the effects, but their directions as well. The direction of an effect determines the direction in which the factors need to be adjusted in a process in order to optimize the process output.

In factorial designs, the main effects are referred to using single uppercase letters, e.g., the main effects of factors A and B are referred to simply as 'A' and 'B', respectively. An interactive effect, on the other hand, is referred to by a group of letters denoting which factors are interacting to produce the effect, e.g., the interactive effect produced by factors A and B is referred to as 'AB'.

Each treatment combination in the experiment is denoted by the lower case letter(s) of the factor(s) that are at 'high' level (or '+' level). Thus, in a 2-factorial experiment, the treatment combinations are: 1) 'a' for the combination wherein factor A = 'high' and factor B = 'low'; 2) 'b' for factor A = 'low' and factor B = 'high'; 3) 'ab' for the combination wherein both A and B = 'high'; and 4) '(1)', which denotes the treatment combination wherein both factors A and B are 'low'.

The main effect of a factor A in a two-level two-factor design is the change in the level of the output produced by a change in the level of A (from 'low' to 'high'), averaged over the two levels of the other factor B. On the other hand, the interaction effect of A and B is the average difference between the effect of A when B is 'high' and the effect of A when B is 'low.' This is also the average difference between the effect of B when A is 'high' and the effect of B when A is 'low.'

The magnitude and polarity (or direction) of the numerical values of main and interaction effects indicate how these effects influence the process output. A higher absolute value for an effect means that the factor responsible for it affects the output significantly. A negative value means that increasing the level(s) of the factor(s) responsible for that effect will decrease the output of the process.

In a 2^2 factorial experiment wherein n replicates were run for each combination treatment, the main and interactive effects of A and B on the output may be mathematically expressed as follows:

A = [ab + a - b - (1)] / 2n;   (main effect of factor A)
B = [ab + b - a - (1)] / 2n;   (main effect of factor B)
AB = [ab + (1) - a - b] / 2n;   (interactive effect of factors A and B)

where n is the number of replicates per treatment combination; a is the total of the outputs of each of the n replicates of the treatment combination a (A is 'high and B is 'low); b is the total output for the n replicates of the treatment combination b (B is 'high' and A is 'low); ab is the total output for the n replicates of the treatment combination ab (both A and B are 'high'); and (1) is the total output for the n replicates of the treatment combination (1) (both A and B are 'low).

The analysis of factor effects in the conduct of 2^k factorial experiments requires a lot of number crunching (even if only two levels per factor are considered in such experiments), especially if the number of factors that are being investigated is high. Fortunately, there's a systematic method for doing the required math in the analysis of factor effects.

The main and interactive effects of A and B in a 2^2 factorial experiment involving n replicates is given as follows: A = [ab + a - b - (1)] / 2n; B = [ab + b - a - (1)] / 2n; and AB = [ab + (1) - a - b] / 2n.

It is to be noted that each of these formulas involves a 'contrast', or a special linear combination of parameters whose coefficients equal zero. For instance, the contrast for A is ab + a − b − 1, while the contrast for B is ab + b − a - 1. The coefficients of A's contrast are -1, +1, -1, and +1 if the contrast were written in what is known as Yates' Order, i.e., ab, a, b, (1). Furthermore, in Yates order, the coefficients of B's contrast are -1, -1, +1, +1 while those of AB's contrast are +1, -1, -1, +1.

The significance of Yates' Order (also known as the 'Standard Order') is that it facilitates the determination of the algebraic signs of the coefficients needed for calculating the main and interaction effects of each factor in a factorial experiment. As discussed earlier, one can easily compute for the numerical values of factor effects if one knows the formulas to use and the output of each replicate for each combination treatment of the factorial experiment. Unfortunately, the formulas look daunting to people not accustomed to them. There is, however, an easy way to reconstruct these formulas using Yates Order.

The secret is in knowing how to list the combination treatments in Yates' Order and how to assign the '+' and '-' signs to them. The Yates order for the combination treatments of 2-factor, 3-factor and 4-factor experiments are:

2 factors: (1), a, b, ab;

3 factors: (1), a, b, ab, c, ac, bc, abc
4 factors: (1), a, b, ab, c, ac, bc, abc, d, ad, bd, abd, cd, acd, bcd, abcd

To facilitate the determination of the algebraic signs of the coefficients needed for calculating the factor effects, one needs to construct a matrix of '+' and '-' signs that map to the factor effects and their combination treatments. The matrix of '+' and '-' signs is usually constructed with the factorial effects forming the column headers and the combination treatments in Yates' Order forming the row headers.

The first rule for filling the matrix with '+' and '-' signs is this: treatment combinations wherein the factor in the column being filled is 'high' will get a '+' sign. On the other hand, treatment combinations wherein that factor is 'low' will get a '-' sign. The second rule is: for interaction factors, the signs of their individual factors simply needs to be multiplied for each treatment. Lastly, the 'identity' column (wherein all factors are 'low') gets a '+' sign for all combination treatments.

Once the matrix is finished, it can be used to look up the algebraic signs of the coefficients of each term in the contrast of each factor, allowing reconstruction of its 'effect' formula. Table 1 shows such a matrix for a 3-factor experiment. Here's an example of how to use this table: to derive the formula for the full effect of factor A, look at the signs under 'A' and assign them to the treatment combinations on their left.

Thus, A = [-(1) + a - b + ab - c + ac - bc + abc]/ 4n.

Table **9:** Algebraic signs - the factor effects in a 23 experiment

Treatment Combination	Factorial Effects							
	I	A	B	AB	C	AC	BC	ABC
(1)	+	-	-	+	-	+	+	-
A	+	+	-	-	-	-	+	+
B	+	-	+	-	-	+	-	+
Ab	+	+	+	+	-	-	-	-
c	+	-	-	+	+	-	-	+
ac	+	+	-	-	+	+	-	-
Bc	+	-	+	-	+	-	+	-
abc	+	+	+	+	+	+	+	+

If there are k factors, each at 2 levels, a full factorial design has 2^k runs.

Full factorial designs are not recommended for 5 or more factors. As shown in the above table, when the number of factors is 5 or greater, a full factorial design requires a large number of runs and is not very efficient.

Example: The example shown below is an independent analysis of a modified portion of the original data set. The original data set was part of a high performance ceramics experiment with the goal of characterizing the effect of grinding parameters on sintered reaction-bonded silicon nitride and sintered silicon nitride.

Only modified data from the first of the 3 ceramic types (sintered reaction-bonded silicon nitride) is discussed in this example of a full factorial data analysis.

Objective: To determine the effect of various machining factors on ceramic strength of response and factor variables used in the experiment.

Response variable = mean (over 15 repetitions) of the ceramic strength.

Number of observations = 32 (a complete 2^5 factorial design).
Response Variable Y = Mean (over 15 reps) of Ceramic Strength.
Factor 1 = Table Speed - 2 levels: slow (.025 m/s) and fast (0.125 m/s).
Factor 2 = Down Feed Rate - 2 levels: slow (.05 mm) and fast (.125 mm).
Factor 3 = Wheel Grit - 2 levels: 140/170 and 80/100.
Factor 4 = Direction - 2 levels: longitudinal and transverse.
Factor 5 = Batch - 2 levels: 1 and 2.

Since two factors were qualitative (direction and batch) and it was reasonable to expect monotone effects from the quantitative factors, no centre point runs were included. The design matrix, with measured ceramic strength responses, is shown below. The actual randomized run order is given in the last column. The software used for doing DoE in this experiment is SAS JMP 3.2.6.

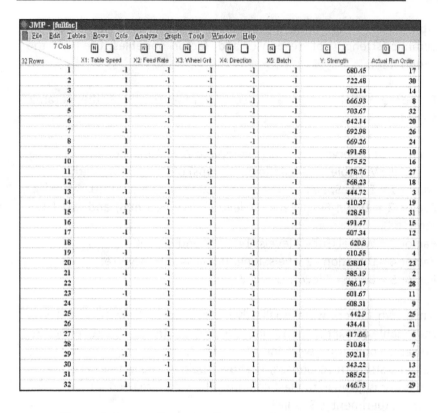

7 Cols	X1: Table Speed	X2: Feed Rate	X3: Wheel Grit	X4: Direction	X5: Batch	Y: Strength	Actual Run Order
32 Rows							
1	-1	-1	-1	-1	-1	680.45	17
2	1	-1	-1	-1	-1	722.48	30
3	-1	1	-1	-1	-1	702.14	14
4	1	1	-1	-1	-1	666.93	8
5	-1	-1	1	-1	-1	703.67	32
6	1	-1	1	-1	-1	642.14	20
7	-1	1	1	-1	-1	692.98	26
8	1	1	1	-1	-1	669.26	24
9	-1	-1	-1	1	-1	491.58	10
10	1	-1	-1	1	-1	475.52	16
11	-1	1	-1	1	-1	478.76	27
12	1	1	-1	1	-1	568.23	18
13	-1	-1	1	1	-1	444.72	3
14	1	-1	1	1	-1	410.37	19
15	-1	1	1	1	-1	428.51	31
16	1	1	1	1	-1	491.47	15
17	-1	-1	-1	-1	1	607.34	12
18	1	-1	-1	-1	1	620.8	1
19	-1	1	-1	-1	1	610.55	4
20	1	1	-1	-1	1	638.04	23
21	-1	-1	1	-1	1	585.19	2
22	1	-1	1	-1	1	586.17	28
23	-1	1	1	-1	1	601.67	11
24	1	1	1	-1	1	608.31	9
25	-1	-1	-1	1	1	442.9	25
26	1	-1	-1	1	1	434.41	21
27	-1	1	-1	1	1	417.66	6
28	1	1	-1	1	1	510.84	7
29	-1	-1	1	1	1	392.11	5
30	1	-1	1	1	1	343.22	13
31	-1	1	1	1	1	385.52	22
32	1	1	1	1	1	446.73	29

Figure **6:** Screen Shot of Full Factorial Experiment in JMP

Analysis of the Experiment

The analysis is done through the following 5 basic steps.

Step 1: Plot the response variable: We start by plotting the response data several ways to see if any trends or anomalies appear that would not be accounted for by the standard linear response models.

First we look at the distribution of all the responses irrespective of factor levels.

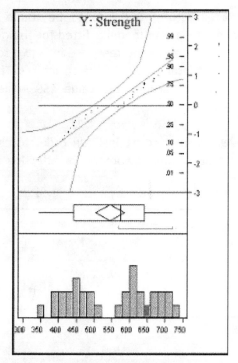

Figure 7: Various plots of the Variables

The following plots were generated:

- The first plot is a normal probability plot of the response variable. The straight red line is the fitted in normal distribution and the curved red lines form a simultaneous 95% confidence region for the plotted points, based on the assumption of normality.
- The second plot is a box plot of the response variable. The 'diamond' is called a "means diamond" and is centered on the sample mean, with endpoints spanning a 95% normal confidence interval for the sample mean.
- The third plot is a histogram of the response variable.

Clearly there is a 'structure' that has to be found out and be accounted for when a response model is fitted for the obtained data. For example, the separation of the response into two roughly equal-sized clumps in the histogram is one of the structures. The first clump is centered approximately around the value 450 while the second clump is present on the 650 region.

Next the responses are plotted against run order to check whether there might be a time sequence component affecting the response levels.

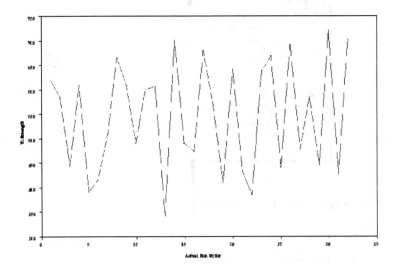

Figure 8: Plot of Response vs. Run Order

As can be seen, this plot does not indicate any significant effect that time order has with response levels.

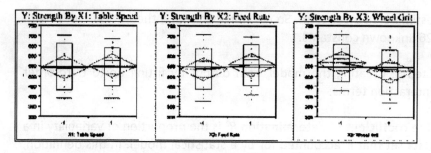

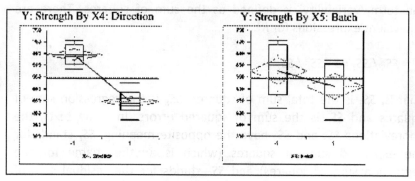

Figure **9:** Box plots of response by factor variables

Several factors, most notably 'direction' followed by 'batch' and possibly "Wheel Grit", appear to change the average response level.

Step 2: Theoretical model (assume all 4-factor and higher interaction terms are not significant) With a 2^5 full factorial experiment a model containing a mean term, all five (5) main effect terms, all ten (10) 2-factor interaction terms, all ten (10) 3-factor interaction terms, all five (5) 4-factor interaction terms and the 5-factor interaction term (32 parameters) can be fitted. However, we start by assuming all three factor and higher interaction terms are non-existent (it is very rare for such high-order interactions to be significant and they are very difficult to interpret from an engineering viewpoint). That allows us to accumulate the sums of squares for these terms and use them to estimate an error term. So we start out with a theoretical model with 26 unknown constants.

Step 3: Creating the model from output by fitting up to third-order interaction terms:

The **coefficient of determination** R^2 is the proportion of variability in a data set that is accounted for by a statistical model. In this definition, the term 'variability' is defined as the sum of squares. There are equivalent expressions for R^2.

$$R^2 = SS_R / SS_T = 1 - SS_E / SS_T$$

That is, SS_T is the total sum of squares, SS_R is the regression sum of squares and SS_E is the sum of squared errors. In some texts, the abbreviations SS_E and SS_R have the opposite meaning: SS_E stands for the explained sum of squares (which is another name for the regression sum of squares) and SS_R stands for the residual sum of squares (another name for the sum of squared errors).

Sum of Squares is defined as the sum of the square of the difference of each term from the mean value. It is also known as the variance.

Total Sum Squares is the sum of the squares of the difference of the dependent variable and its grand mean.

Total sum of squares = explained sum of squares + residual sum of squares.
R-square is the statistic that will give information about the goodness of fit of the model. R-square increases as we increase the number of variables in the model (R-square will not decrease), so the alternative technique is to look for adjusted R-square. The explanation of this

statistic is also same as R-square but it penalizes R-square by the number of variables used in the model.

The coefficient of determination R^2 is a measure of the global fit of the model. Specifically, R^2 is an element of [0, 1] and represents the proportion of variability in Y_i that may be attributed to some linear combination of the regressors (explanatory variables) in X.

Thus, $R^2 = 1$ indicates that the fitted model explains all variability in y, while $R^2 = 0$ indicates no 'linear' relationship between the response variable and regressors. An interior value such as $R^2 = 0.7$ may be interpreted as follows: Approximately seventy percent of the variation in the response variable can be explained by the explanatory variable.

Adjusted R^2 is a modification of R^2 that adjusts for the number of explanatory terms in a model. Unlike R^2, the adjusted R^2 increases only if the new term improves the model more than would be expected by chance. The adjusted R^2 can be negative and will always be less than or equal to R^2.

Adjusted R^2 is not always *better* than R^2: adjusted R^2 will be more useful only if the R^2 is calculated based on a sample, not the entire population.

The F-ratio is used to determine whether the variances in two independent samples are equal.

$F = S_1^2 / S_2^2$ where,
S_1 = largest variance
S_2 = smallest variance
DF- Degrees of Freedom

After fitting the 26 parameter model, the following analysis table is displayed:

Summary of Fit

Output after Fitting Third Order Model to Response Data
Response: Y: Strength

R-Square	0.995127
R-Square Adjusted	0.974821
Root Mean Square Error	17.81632
Mean of Response	546.8959
Observations	32

Table 10: Effect Test

Test #	Source	DF	Sum of Squares	F (Ratio)	Prob > F
1	X1: Table Speed	1	894.33	2.8175	0.1442
2	X2: Feed Rate	1	3497.2	11.0175	0.016
3	X1: Table Speed*X2: Feed Rate	1	4872.57	15.3505	0.0078
4	X3: Wheel Grit	1	12663.96	39.8964	0.0007
5	X1: Table Speed*X3: Wheel Grit	1	1838.76	5.7928	0.0528
6	X2: Feed Rate*X3: Wheel Grit	1	307.46	0.9686	0.363
7	X1:Table Speed*X2: Feed Rate*X3: Wheel Grit	1	357.05	1.1248	0.3297
8	X4: Direction	1	315132.65	992.7901	< 0.0001
9	X1: Table Speed*X4: Direction	1	1637.21	5.1578	0.0636
10	X2: Feed Rate*X4: Direction	1	1972.71	6.2148	0.047
11	X1: Table Speed	1	5895.62	18.5735	0.005
12	X2: Feed Rate*X4: Direction	1	1972.71	6.2148	0.047
13	X3: Wheel Grit*X4: Direction	1	3158.34	9.95	0.0197
14	X1: Table Speed*X3: Wheel Grit*X4: Direction	1	2.12	0.0067	0.9376
15	X2: Feed Rate*X3: Wheel Grit*X4: Direction	1	44.49	0.1401	0.721

16	X5: Batch	1	33653.91	106.0229	< 0.1
17	X1: Table Speed*X5: Batch	1	465.05	1.4651	0.2716
18	X2: Feed Rate*X5: Batch	1	199.15	0.6274	0.4585
19	X1: Table Speed*X2: Feed Rate*X5: Batch	1	144.71	0.4559	0.5247
20	X3: Wheel Grit*X5: Batch	1	29.36	0.0925	0.7713
21	X1: Table Speed*X3: Wheel Grit*X5: Batch	1	30.36	0.0957	0.7676
22	X2: Feed Rate*X3: Wheel Grit*X5: Batch	1	25.58	0.0806	0.786
23	X4: Direction *X5: Batch	1	1328.83	4.1863	0.867
24	X1: Table Speed*X4: Direction *X5: Batch	1	544.58	1	0.2382
25	X2: Feed Rate*X4: Direction*X5: Batch	1	167.31	0.5271	0.4952
26	X3: Wheel Grit*X4: Direction*X5: Batch	1	32.46	0.1023	0.76

This fit has a high R^2 and adjusted R^2, but the large number of high (>0.10) p-values (in the "Prob>F" column) make it clear that the model has many unnecessary terms.

JMP stepwise regression: Starting with these 26 terms, we next use the JMP Stepwise Regression option to eliminate unnecessary terms. By a combination of stepwise regression and the removal of remaining terms with a p-value higher than 0.05, we quickly arrive at a model with an intercept and 12 significant effect terms.

Output after Fitting the 12-Term Model to Response Data
Response: Y: Strength

Summary of Fit

R Square	0.989114
R Square Adjusted	0.982239
Root Mean Square Error	14.96346
Mean of Response	546.8959

Observations   32

Table **11:** Effect Test after Stepwise Regression

Test #	Source	DF	Sum of Squares	F (Ratio)	Prob> F
1	X1: Table Speed	1	894.33	2.8175	0.1442
2	X2: Feed Rate	1	3497.2	11.0175	0.016
3	X1: Table Speed*X2: Feed Rate	1	4872.57	15.3505	0.0078
4	X3: Wheel Grit	1	12663.96	39.8964	0.0007
5	X1: Table Speed*X3: Wheel Grit	1	1838.76	5.7928	0.0528
8	X4: Direction	1	315132.65	992.7901	< 0.0001
9	X1: Table Speed*X4: Direction	1	1637.21	5.1578	0.0636
10	X2: Feed Rate*X4: Direction	1	1972.71	6.2148	0.047
11	X1: Table Speed	1	5895.62	18.5735	0.005
13	X3: Wheel Grit*X4: Direction	1	3158.34	9.95	0.0197
16	X5: Batch	1	33653.91	106.0229	< 0.1
23	X4: Direction *X5: Batch	1	1328.83	4.1863	0.867

Normal plot of the effects: Non-significant effects should effectively follow an approximately normal distribution with the same location and scale. Significant effects will vary from this normal distribution. Therefore, another method of determining significant effects is to generate a normal plot of all 31 effects (since X4 and X5 are too large for scale, the combined effect of five factors or five factor interactions are not considered). Those effects that are substantially away from the straight line fitted to the normal plot are considered significant. Although this is a somewhat a subjective criteria, it tends to work well in practice. It is helpful to use both the numerical output from the fit and graphical techniques such as the normal plot in deciding which terms to keep in the model.

The normal plot of the effects is shown below. We have labeled those effects that we consider to be significant. In this case, we have arrived at the exact same 12 terms by looking at the normal plot as we did from the stepwise regression.

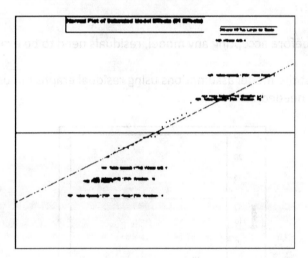

Figure **10**: Normal Plot of Saturated Model Effects

Most of the effects cluster close to the center (zero) line and follow the fitted normal model straight line. The effects that appear to be above or below the line by more than a small amount are the same effects identified using the stepwise routine, with the exception of $X1$. Some analysts prefer to include a main effect term when it has several significant interactions even if the main effect term itself does not appear to be significant.

Model appears to account for most of the variability: At this stage, this model appears to account for most of the variability in the response, achieving an adjusted R^2 of 0.982. All the main effects are significant, as are 6 two-factor interactions and 1 three-factor interaction. The only interaction that makes little physical sense is the " $X4$: Direction*$X5$: Batch" interaction - why would the response using one batch of material react differently when the batch is cut in a different direction as compared to another batch of the same formulation?

However, before accepting any model, residuals need to be examined.

Step 4: Test the model assumptions using residual graphs (adjust and simplify as needed).

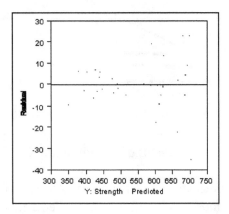

Figure **11:** Plot of residuals versus predicted

The residuals appear to spread out more with larger values of predicted strength, which should not happen when there is a common variance.

Next we examine the normality of the residuals with a normal quintile plot, a box plot and a histogram.

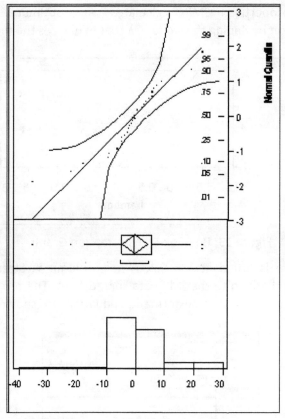

Figure **12**: Normality of the residuals

None of these plots appear to show typical normal residuals and 4 of the 32 data points appear as outliers in the box plot.

Step 4 continued: Transform the data and fit the model again.

Box-Cox Transformation: We next look at whether we can model a transformation of the response variable and obtain residuals with the assumed properties. JMP calculates an optimum Box-Cox transformation by finding the value of λ that minimizes the model SS_E.

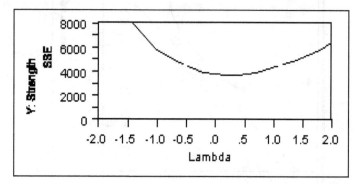

Figure **13**: Box-Cox Transformation Graph

The optimum is found at $\lambda = 0.2$. A new column Y: Strength X is calculated and added to the JMP data spreadsheet. The properties of this column, showing the transformation equation, are shown below:

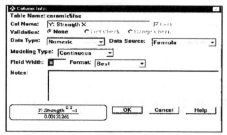

Figure 14: **Data Transformation Column Properties**

Fit model to transformed data: When the 12-effect model is fit to the transformed data, the "X4: Direction*X5: Batch" interaction term becomes no longer significant. The 11-effect model fit is shown below, with parameter estimates and *p*-values.

Output after Fitting the 11-Effect Model to Transformed Response Data
Response: Y: Strength X

Summary of Fit

R-Square	0.99041
R-Square Adjusted	0.985135
Root Mean Square Error	13.81065
Mean of Response	1917.115
No. of Observations	32

Table 12: 11 Effect Model Data

#	Effect	Parameter Estimate	p-value
	Intercept	1917.115	<.0001
1	X1: Table Speed	5.777	0.0282
2	X2: Feed Rate	11.691	0.0001
3	X1: Table Speed*X2: Feed Rate	-14.467	<.0001
4	X3: Wheel Grit	-21.649	<.0001
5	X1: Table Speed*X3: Wheel Grit	7.339	0.007
6	X4: Direction	-99.272	<.0001
7	X1: Table Speed*X4: Direction	-7.188	0.008
8	X2: Feed Rate*X4: Direction	-9.16	0.0013
9	X1: Table Speed*X2: Feed Rate*X4:Direction	15.325	<.0001
10	X3: Wheel Grit*X4: DirectionX5: Batch	12.965	<.0001
11	X5: Batch	-31.871	<.0001

Model has high R²: This model has a very high R^2 and adjusted R^2. The residual plots (shown below) are quite a bit better behaved than before and pass the Wilk-Shapiro test for normality.

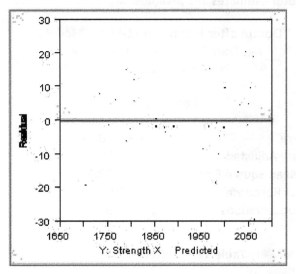

Figure **15**: Residual plots – model with transformed response

The run sequence plot of the residuals does not indicate any time dependent patterns.

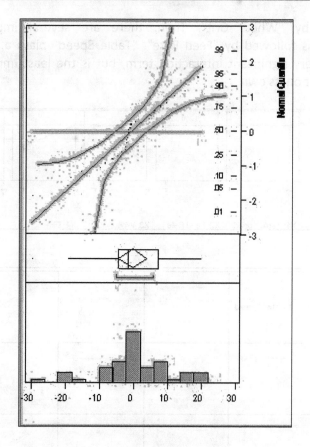

Figure **16:** Normal probability, box plot & residuals

The normal probability plot, box plot and the histogram of the residuals do not indicate any serious violations of the model assumptions.

Step 5: Important main effects and interaction effects: The magnitudes of the effect estimates show that 'Direction' is by far the most important factor. 'Batch' plays the next most critical role, followed by "Wheel Grit". Then, there are several important interactions followed by "Feed Rate". "Table Speed" plays a role in almost every significant interaction term, but is the least important main effect on its own.

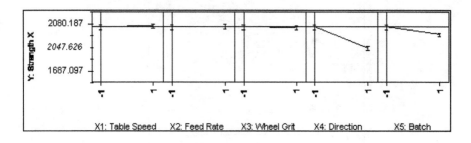

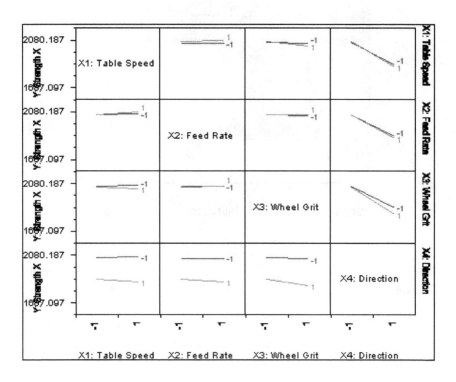

Y: Strength X
Prediction Profile

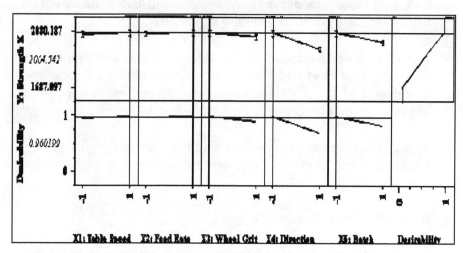

Figure **17:** Main effects plot & significant 2-way interactions

The vertical lines indicate the optimal factor settings to maximize the (transformed) strength response. Translating from -1 and +1 back to the actual factor settings, we have: Table speed at '1' or 0.125m/s; Down Feed Rate at '1' or 0.125 mm; Wheel Grit at '-1' or 140/170 and Direction at '-1' or longitudinal.

Unfortunately, 'Batch' is also a very significant factor, with the first batch giving higher strengths than the second. Unless it is possible to learn what worked well with this batch and how to repeat it, not much can be done about this factor.

Analysis with value of Direction fixed indicates complex model is needed only for transverse cut

One might ask what an analysis of just the 2^4 factorial with 'Direction' kept at -1 (i.e., longitudinal) would yield. This analysis turns out to have a very simple model; only "Wheel Grit" and 'Batch' are significant main effects and no interactions are significant.

If, on the other hand, we do an analysis of the 2^4 factorial with 'Direction' kept at +1 (i.e., transverse), then we obtain a 7-parameter model with all the main effects and interactions we saw in the 2^5 analysis, except, of course, any terms involving 'Direction'.

So it appears that the complex model of the full analysis came from the physical properties of a transverse cut and these complexities are not present for longitudinal cuts.

4.4.5.3 Fractional Factorial Designs

Fractional factorial is defined as a factorial experiment in which only an adequately chosen fraction of the treatment combinations required for the complete factorial experiment is selected to be run.

Even if the number of factors, k, in a design is small, the 2^k runs specified for a full factorial can quickly become very large. For example, $2^6 = 64$ runs for a two-level full factorial design with six factors. To this design we need to add a good number of center-point runs and we can thus quickly run up a very large resource requirement for runs with only a modest number of factors. The right fraction for 2-level designs has to be chosen for it to be both balanced and orthogonal. The solution to this problem is to use only a fraction of the runs specified by the full factorial design. The runs to be made and to be left out, is the subject of interest here. In general, we pick a fraction such as ½, ¼, etc. of the runs called for by the full factorial. We use various strategies that ensure an appropriate choice of runs.

Properly chosen fractional factorial designs for 2-level experiments have the desirable properties of being both balanced and orthogonal.

The emphasis will be laid only on fractions of two-level designs because two-level fractional designs are by far the most popular fractional designs.

Fractional Factorial designs are also known as orthogonal type of design as they make use of orthogonal arrays extensively. It is the most important type of design as there is maximum test coverage with minimum number of experiments for a given number of factors and levels.

To define an orthogonal array, the following factors have to be considered:

- Number of factors to be studied
- Levels for each factor
- The specific 2-factor interactions to be estimated
- The special difficulties that would be encountered in running the experiment

Orthogonal array enables good test coverage with less number of test cases than the exhaustive testing strategy. It can give an efficient result by using only 27 test cases against a possible 1,594,000 test cases in one of the experiments if the factors and the levels are properly chosen. The following table illustrates the limitations of the other conventional testing case design methods as compared to the orthogonal arrays.

Table **13**: Conventional designs vs. original array designs

Test Case Design based on	Testing efforts	Ability to Find Faults	Advantages/ Limitations
Random/Intuitive (Based on Past History)	Medium	Unpredictable	As the fault finding is unpredictable. Testing by this method is a blind search. Poor Test Coverage
One at a Time	Small	Limited	Takes a long time and has poor test coverage
Exhaustive Testing	Very Large	All Faults Found (100%)	Takes a long time to execute all test cases and it directly increases the cost. Has good test coverage
Orthogonal Array	Small	Near 100% coverage and far superior compared to random and one at a time.	Helps in cost effective test coverage.

Here is an example of an orthogonal array of strength 2:

Table **14**: Orthogonal Array of Strength 2

0	0	0	0	0	0	0	0	0	0	0
1	1	1	0	1	1	0	1	0	0	0
0	1	1	1	0	1	1	0	1	0	0
0	0	1	1	1	0	1	1	0	1	0
0	0	0	1	1	1	0	1	1	0	1
1	0	0	0	1	1	1	0	1	1	0
0	1	0	0	0	1	1	1	0	1	1
1	0	1	0	0	0	1	1	1	0	1
1	1	0	1	0	0	0	1	1	1	0
0	1	1	0	1	0	0	0	1	1	1
1	0	1	1	0	1	0	0	0	1	1
1	1	0	1	1	0	1	0	0	0	1

Pick any two columns; say the first and the last:

0	0
1	0
0	0
0	0
0	1
1	0
0	1
1	1
1	0
0	1
1	1
1	1

Each of the four possible rows we might see in this is:

0 0,   0 1,   1 0,   1 1,

and they all appear **the same number of times** (three times, in fact).

That is the property that makes it an orthogonal array.

Only 0's and 1's appear in that array, but for use in statistics it is used as

0   or   1

The first column might be replaced by

"sugar"   or   "no sugar"

or

"slow cooling"	or	"fast cooling"
"catalyst"	or	"no catalyst"

and hence on depending on the application.

Since only 0's and 1's appear, this is called a **2-level array**. There are 11 columns, which mean we can vary the levels of **11 different variables** and 12 rows, which means we are going to bake 12 different cakes, or produce **12 different samples** of the alloy. In short, we call this array an **OA(12, 11, 2, 2).**

The first '2' indicates the number of levels and the second '2' the **strength**, which is the number of columns where we are guaranteed to see all the possibilities an equal number of times. In the above experiment we can see the above mentioned four possible combinations for three times each at a time in taking two columns. So its strength is two. In an orthogonal array of strength 3 (with two levels), in any **three** columns we would see each of the eight possibilities

000, 001, 010, 011, 100, 101, 110, 111

equally often.

As already mentioned, the main applications of orthogonal arrays are in planning experiments. The rows of the array represent the experiments or tests to be performed - cakes to be baked, samples of alloy to be produced, integrated circuits to be etched, test plots of crops to be grown and so on.

The columns of the orthogonal array correspond to the different variables whose effects are being analyzed. The entries in the array specify the levels at which the variables are to be applied. If a row of the orthogonal array reads

110100 ...

this could mean that in that test the first, second, fourth variables (where the 1's occur) are to be set at their 'high' levels and the third, fifth, sixth variables (where the 0's occur) at their 'low' levels.

By basing the experiment on an orthogonal array of strength 't' we ensure that all possible combinations of up to 't' of the variables occur together equally often.

The aim here is to investigate not only the effects of the individual variables (or factors) on the outcome, but also how the variables interact. Obviously, even with a moderate number of factors and a small number of levels for each factor, the number of possible level combinations for the factors increases rapidly. It may therefore not be feasible to make even one observation at each of the level combinations. In such cases observations are made at only some of the level combinations and the purpose of the orthogonal array is to specify which level combinations are to be used. Such experiments are called "fractional factorial" experiments. While there are nowadays other applications of orthogonal arrays in statistics (for example in computer experiments and survey sampling), the principal application is in the selection of level combinations for fractional factorial experiments.

Since the rows of an orthogonal array represent runs (or tests or samples) - which require money, time and other resources - there are always practical constraints on the number of rows that can be used in an experiment. Finding the smallest possible number of rows is a problem of eminent importance. On the other hand, for a given number of runs we may want to know the largest number of columns that can be used in an orthogonal array, since this will tell us how many variables can be studied. We also want the strength to be large, though in many real-life applications this is set at 2, 3 or 4.

Factors, levels, the number of Test Cases and Selecting Orthogonal Array for Test Case Design:

Even at the cost of duplication, for completeness sake some major parameters are defined here:

Orthogonal arrays are generic experimental models. Factors, Levels and number of experiments are the three important concepts in orthogonal arrays. Understanding, these concepts will help in applying orthogonal arrays for designing test cases.

The **need for Orthogonal Array** – One of the challenges in testing this application was that the conventional method of analytical and functional testing was not sufficient to provide adequate test coverage as the number of combinations to test was quite huge and it would not be practically possible to exhaust all possible cases. It has 13 factors each varying between 3 levels thus giving us **1594323 (3^{13}) test cases** to be tested in the case of exhaustive testing. Hence by making use of OA, a more scientific technique, it has been effectively reduced to **27 test cases** and also found the testing to be successful.

Approach to test case design – Coarse testing is done in the initial stages, called analytical testing using the 'white box' approach to cover only the important logics and to create a stable application. A stable application and testing environment is ensured at this stage. Only 25% of the total testing effort is exhausted at this stage. The next stage of testing focuses on finer details, called the functional testing using a 'black box' approach with Orthogonal Array (OA), which improves test coverage. This helps in identifying specific faulty areas in the application in question.

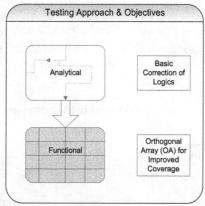

Figure 18 - Approach to test case design

A **factor** is a variable under study (mathematically x, y, z axis for 3 factors); an input that can be controlled. As an example, in a data entry form, one of the fields may constitute a factor. A factor can be either quantitative or qualitative.

A **level** is a value that a factor can assume (mathematically values of x, y, z coordinates) when used in an experiment. In the example of a data entry form cited above, levels can be the possible values for the field. Although the field accepts many different values, boundary values are taken to stimulate extreme conditions.

The **process flow** has to be understood thoroughly in designing test cases as it is the foundation in testing. In this case study the initial step is to do analytical testing and check whether the application is stable and then do functional testing, where the factors and levels were identified, the orthogonal array chosen and the test cases generated.

The **selection of orthogonal array** is done based on the number of factors (variables) under study and their levels (possible values) to which the testing should be done. Orthogonal Array selected dictates the number of test cases which needs to be tested Table 15 lists the important orthogonal arrays available for selection.

Table **15**: List of important orthogonal arrays

Orthogonal Array	Number of Test Cases	No of Factors	Max no of Factors at these levels			
			2 Levels	3 Levels	4 Levels	5 Levels
L-4	4	3	3	-	-	-
L-8	8	7	7	-	-	-
L-9	9	4	-	4	-	-
L-12	12	11	11	-	-	-
L-16	16	15	15	-	-	-
L-'16	16	5		-	5	-
L-18	18	8	1	7	-	-
L-25	25	6	-	-	-	6
L-27	27	13	-	13	-	-
L-32	32	31	31	-	-	-
L-'32	32	10	1	-	9	-
L-36	36	23	11	12	-	-
L-'36	36	16	3	13	-	

Orthogonal Array	Number of Test Cases	No of Factors	Max no of Factors at these levels			
			2 Levels	3 Levels	4 Levels	5 Levels
L-50	50	12	1	-	-	11
L-54	54	26	1	25	-	-
L-64	64	63	63	-	-	-
L-'64	64	21	-	-	21	-
L-81	81	40	-	40	-	-

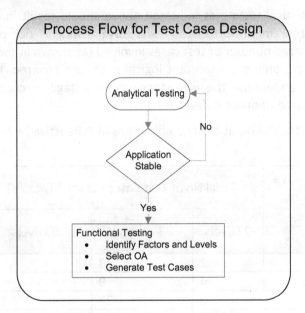

Figure **19**: Steps in Designing Test Cases

Analytical Testing:

Developers use a pragmatic approach to unit test and debug the application. Unit testing including - Basic path testing, Conditional testing, Data flow testing and Loop testing. Since the developers are conversant with the source code, maximum benefit that can be derived from a 'white box' approach is achieved, resulting in a stable application free of major defects and show stoppers.

Ideally, analytical testing as indicated above should result in a 100% bug-free program. Unfortunately exhaustive testing is not practical due to the large number of test cases involved (as shown in the above table). Hence, only the important logical paths are covered, but this should not undermine the importance of this stage in creating an application free of major defects.

Table **16:** The number of combinations in Exhaustive testing

Exhaustive Testing	Total No of Test Cases (Level ^ Factors)		
No of Factors	2 Levels	3 Levels	5 Levels
1	2	3	5
2	4	9	25
3	8	27	125
4	16	81	625
5	32	243	3125
6	64	729	15625
7	128	2187	78125
8	256	6561	390625
9	512	19683	1953125
10	1024	59049	9765625

Exhaustive Testing	Total No of Test Cases (Level ^ Factors)		
No of Factors	2 Levels	3 Levels	5 Levels
11	2048	177147	48828125
12	4096	531441	244140625
13	8192	1594323	1220703125
14	16384	4782969	6103515625
15	32768	14348907	30517578125

Functional Testing:

From a pragmatic approach we move to a scientific approach which is taken to generate test cases that give maximum coverage from a functional point of view. This is done by an exclusive "**Testing Team**".

The testing team identifies all the functional requirements (equivalent to factors in Orthogonal Arrays) of the applications which need to be tested at various values (equivalent to levels in Orthogonal Arrays). As said earlier the selection of Orthogonal Array is done based on the number of functions (factors) and their values (level).

Based on the selected Orthogonal Array the Test Cases design is generated. A simple Visual Basic Application having a data base of orthogonal arrays can be used in accurately generating test case designs. Testing is done to identify the faulty locations.

Example:

Let us consider an example of testing copy machine functionality for test parameters and levels. Here, parameter A could be number of original papers and levels being 1 paper, 10 papers or 51 papers.

Parameter B could be Duplex with levels being one-sided copy or two-sided etc. as shown in Table 1. The optimal or the most efficient values of these parameters have to be found out.

Table **17:** Parameters And Levels

Test Parameters	Level 1	Level 2	Level 3
A. Number of Originals	1	10	51
B. Duplex	1 to 1	1 to 2	2 to 2
C. Collating	None	Yes	Stapled
D. Interrupt	None	Panel	Tray

4.5 Orthogonal Array (OA) -Based Test Cases

Below table shows the test plan using OA (Orthogonal Array) L9. It has nine rows and four columns. The rows correspond to test cases; the columns correspond to the test parameters. Thus, the first test case comprises Level 1 for each parameter, i.e., it represents the combination A1, B1, C1, D1. The second test case comprises combination A1, B2, C2, D2, etc.

Table 18: Test Plan Using OA L9

Test #	No. of Originals	Duplex	Collating	Interrupt
1	1	1 to 1	None	None
2	1	1 to 2	Yes	Panel
3	1	2 to 2	Stapled	Tray
4	10	1 to 1	Yes	Tray
5	10	1 to 2	Stapled	None
6	10	2 to 2	None	Panel
7	51	1 to 1	Stapled	Panel

Test #	No. of Originals	Duplex	Collating	Interrupt
8	51	1 to 2	None	Tray
9	51	2 to 2	Yes	None

An orthogonal array has the balancing property that, for each pair of columns, all parameter-level combinations occur an equal number of times. In OA L9, there are nine parameter-level combinations for each pair of columns and each combination occurs once.

By conducting the nine tests indicated by L9, we can accomplish the following:

- Detect and isolate all single-mode faults. A single-mode fault is a consistent problem with any level of any single parameter. For example, if all cases of factor A at Level A1 cause error condition, it is a single-mode failure. In this example, tests 1, 2 and 3 will show errors. By analyzing the information about which tests show error, one can identify which factor level causes the fault. In this example, by noting that the tests 1, 2 and 3 cause an error, one can isolate A1 as the source of the fault. Such an isolation of fault is important to fix the fault.

- Detect all double-mode faults. If there exists a problem which is consistent and also wherein specific levels of two parameters occur together, it is called a double-mode fault. Indeed, a double-mode fault is an indication of pair-wise incompatibility or harmful interactions between two test parameters.

Multimode faults: OAs of strength 2 can assure the detection of only the single- and double-mode faults. However, many multimode faults are also detected by these tests. This can be understood by studying the interaction tables and the geometric view of the test cases presented in the next section.

Geometric View of Test Cases

Software faults can be divided into two categories: region faults and isolated faults, as shown in figure. Faults that occur for only one specific combination of test parameter levels, such as by a data-entry error, are called isolated faults. Assurance against isolated faults is not possible without testing all combinations. However, when the logic is faulty, there is a tendency for a region of the test domain to exhibit malfunction. Such faults are called region faults. Single-mode and double-mode faults are special cases of region faults. Orthogonal Array based testing is highly effective for the detection of region faults with a relatively small number of tests.

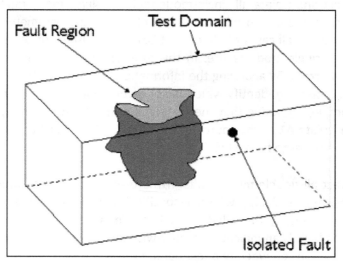

Figure **20**: Region Faults And Isolated Faults

A geometric picture of the test cases can provide an insight into the benefits of OA-based test cases in the detection of region faults. To facilitate geometric visualization, take the example of software with only three test parameters A, B and C. The test domain is cube-shaped and consists of 27 lattice points. Test cases based on the OA L9 and those based on the one-factor-at-a-time method are graphically displayed in the following figure. The OA-based test cases are dispersed uniformly throughout the test domain.

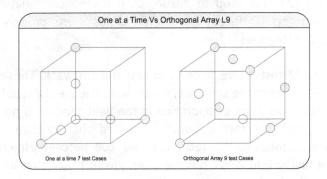

Figure 21: Comparison of OVAT & L9 OA design

4.5.1   A Case Study

A comprehensive case study of orthogonal array based testing was published by AT&T in 1992. The study detailed regression testing of a PC (IBM format) and local area network-based electronic mail software called StarMail. Originally, a test plan was prepared that consisted of 1,500 tests that would take 18 weeks to conduct. However, because of development delays, the testing time had to be cut short to only eight weeks. The lead test engineer had, therefore, prepared an alternate plan involving 1,000 tests that would take two people eight weeks. But he was unsure about the quality of testing, i.e., its ability to detect all faults. To alleviate these problems, a test plan was prepared using the orthogonal array based Robust Testing method.

The Robust Testing method began with the division of the functions of the StarMail software into 18 categories, test parameters and levels for each category were found and an OA to select test cases for each category was used. For example, for the copy/move function, the selected OA L27 was used to ensure all pair-wise combinations of these parameters. Different parameter tables were prepared for remaining 17 categories.

In all, only 422 tests were needed to test the software. These tests identified 41 faults in the software, which were fixed and the software was released. Two years of operation in the field generated no faults within the scope of testing, which indicated that relative to the scenarios encountered, the test plan was 100 percent effective in identifying faults. Had AT&T run the alternate test plan that involved 1,000 tests, the lead tester estimated they may have found only 32 of the 41 faults. Compared to the original testing plan, Robust Testing required 50 percent less testing effort, identified 28 percent more faults and was more productive (number of faults detected per tester week) by a factor of 2^6.

Regression Testing

Orthogonal array based testing is very useful in regression testing. After fixing the faults, one can easily prepare a new test plan using array rotation technique.

Table **19**: New Regression Test Plan

Test #	Duplex	Collating	Interrupt	No. of Originals
1	1 to 1	None	None	1
2	1 to 1	Yes	Panel	10
3	1 to 1	Stapled	Tray	51
4	1 to 2	None	Panel	51
5	1 to 2	Yes	Tray	1
6	1 to 2	Stapled	None	10

Test #	Duplex	Collating	Interrupt	No. of Originals
7	2 to 2	None	Tray	10
8	2 to 2	Yes	None	51
9	2 to 2	Stapled	Panel	1

A lot of time, energy and cost savings are available during this phase.

In general the required number of test cases would be - x such that $Q^x > P$

Where Q is the number of levels of the factor and P is the number of factors.

For instance $2^3 > 4$ gives us that for a test case with 4 factors each having 2 different levels the required number of test cases $= 8 = 2^3$ where as it would require 16 (2^4) test cases by full factorial method.

The levels for each factor for each test run for different Orthogonal Arrays were devised by Taguchi. Some of the very basic tables are given below.

Table 20: L4- for 3 factors at 2 levels

Experiment #	Column		
	1	2	3
1	1	1	1
2	1	2	2
3	2	1	2
4	2	2	1

Table **21:** L8 for 7 factors at 2 levels

Experiment #	Column						
	1	**2**	**3**	**4**	**5**	**6**	**7**
1	1	1	1	1	1	1	1
2	1	1	1	2	2	2	2
3	1	2	2	1	1	2	2
4	1	2	2	2	2	1	1
5	2	1	2	1	2	1	2
6	2	1	2	2	1	2	1
7	2	2	1	1	2	2	1
8	2	2	1	2	1	1	2

Table 22: L9 for 4 factors at 3 levels

Experiment #	Column			
	1	**2**	**3**	**4**
1	1	1	1	1
2	1	2	2	2
3	1	3	3	3
4	2	1	2	3
5	2	2	3	1
6	2	3	1	2
7	3	1	3	2
8	3	2	1	3
9	3	3	2	1

Table 23: L12 for 11 factors at 2 levels

Experiment #	Column										
	1	2	3	4	5	6	7	8	9	10	11
1	1	1	1	1	1	1	1	1	1	1	1
2	1	1	1	1	1	2	2	2	2	2	2
3	1	1	2	2	2	1	1	1	2	2	2
4	1	2	1	2	2	1	2	2	1	1	2
5	1	2	2	1	2	2	1	2	1	2	1
6	1	2	2	2	1	2	2	1	2	1	1
7	2	1	2	2	1	1	2	2	1	2	1
8	2	1	2	1	2	2	2	1	1	1	2
9	2	1	1	2	2	2	1	2	2	1	1
10	2	2	2	1	1	1	1	2	2	1	2
11	2	2	1	2	1	2	1	1	1	2	2
12	2	2	1	1	2	1	2	1	2	2	1

The major advantages of using Orthogonal Arrays are

1. Conclusions are valid over the entire region spanned by the control factors and their settings
2. Large saving in the experimental effort
3. Analysis is easy

4.6 Response Surface Methodology (RSM)

Response Surface Methodology (RSM) is an experimental strategy consisting of a particular set of mathematical and statistical methods. The RSM uses quantitative data from appropriate experimental designs to determine and simultaneously solve multivariate equations graphically represented as response surfaces which can be used in three ways:

1.   To describe how the test variables affect the response
2.   To determine the interrelationships among the test variables
3.   To describe the combined effect of all test variables on the response.

For product development, RSM can be used to establish the optimum level of the primary ingredients in a product, once these ingredients have been identified. This information helps the product developer to understand ingredient interactions in the product which guide final product formulation and future cost and quality changes. The optimization procedure for product development has been found to save time, ultimately cost less than repeated consumer testing of one or two products at a time and provide a level of certainty about the performance of the product formulation. Similarly, in process development the processing parameters can be optimized by using a minimum number of experimental steps by selecting a suitable experimental design. This presentation will give an overview of RSM and elaborate a 15-point step-by-step approach for utilizing RSM techniques in process and product optimization. The speaker will take three diverse examples from the research conducted in his lab to illustrate RSM-based optimization. These examples relate to optimizing a vegetable lye peeling process, optimizing a peanut butter formulation and using a mixture design approach in optimizing ingredient levels in developing a formulation.

The different types of Response Surface Methodologies are

- Central Composite
- Box-Behnken
- Contour Plots
- Mesh Plots
- Multiple Linear Regression
- Stepwise Regression

4.7 Conclusion:

Thus **Design of Experiment** involves designing a set of ten to twenty experiments, in which all relevant factors are varied systematically. When the results of these experiments are analyzed, they help to identify optimal conditions, the factors that most influence the results and those that do not, as well as details such as the existence of interactions and synergies between factors.

When DoE applied to a well-structured matrix, analysis of variance delivers accurate results, even when the matrix that is analyzed is quite small. Today, Fisher's methods of design and analysis are international standards in business and applied science.

Building a design means, carefully choosing a small number of experiments that are to be performed under controlled conditions.

There are four interrelated steps in building a design:

1. Define an objective to the investigation, e.g. better understand or sort out important variables or find optimum.
2. Define the variables that will be controlled during the experiment (design variables) and their levels or ranges of variation.
3. Define the variables that will be measured to describe the outcome of the experimental runs (response variables) and examine their precision.
4. Among the available standard designs, choose the one that is compatible with the objective, number of design variables and precision of measurements and has a reasonable cost.

Standard designs are well-known classes of experimental designs. They can be generated automatically as soon as the objective has been decided, the number and nature of design variables, the nature of the responses and the number of experimental runs that can afforded. Generating such a design will provide with a list of all experiments that must performed, to gather enough information for the required purposes.

Design of Experiments (DoE) is widely used in research and development, where a large proportion of the resources go towards solving optimization problems. The key to minimizing optimization costs is to conduct as few experiments as possible. DoE requires only a small set of experiments and thus helps to reduce costs.

Design of Experiments (DoE) is a more complete method when compared to One Variable at a Time method as it also takes into account the interaction between the variables or factors also.

*****

Chapter 5 - Quality Control and Taguchi Methods

Now, more than ever before, processing costs and problems of repeatability can stall new composite programs right at the profit line. Marginal improvements in the control of composites manufacturing processes, although useful in the short term, will not provide the needed levels of quality, reliability, or economy of production. Figure below depicts the shift in approaches used to ensure product quality as a function of time. Taguchi methods belong to the class of approaches that attempt to ensure quality through design, in this case through the identification and control of critical variables (or noises) that cause deviations to occur in the process/ product quality.

Taguchi methods, developed by Dr. Genichi Taguchi, refer to techniques of quality engineering that embody both Statistical Process Control (SPC) and new quality related management techniques. Most of the attention and discussion on Taguchi methods has been focused on the statistical aspects of the procedure; it is the conceptual framework of a methodology for quality improvement and process robustness that needs to be emphasized.

The entire concept can be described in two basic ideas:

- Quality should be measured by the deviation from a specified target value, rather than by conformance to preset tolerance limits.
- Quality cannot be ensured through inspection and rework, but must be built in through the appropriate design of the process and product.

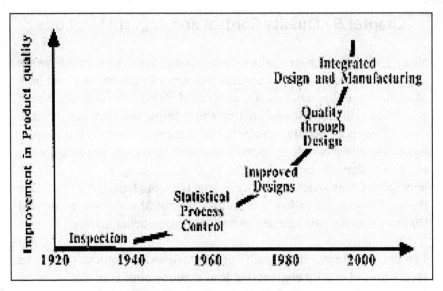

Figure **22**: The Evolution of Quality Control

The first concept underlines the basic difference between Taguchi methods and the SPC methodology. Whereas SPC methods emphasize the attainment of an attribute within a tolerance range and are used to check product/ process quality, Taguchi methods emphasize the attainment of the specified target value and the elimination of variation. In conjunction with the second concept, this assumes great significance for composites manufacturing since Taguchi methods emphasize that control factors must be optimized to make them insensitive to manufacturing transients through design, rather than by trial and error. SPC allows for faults and defects to be eliminated (when detected) after manufacture, whereas what is really needed is a methodology that prevents their occurrence. In this case, the methodology is the use of Taguchi methods. This then presents a powerful tool for composites processing within which there is an inherent variability due to raw material quality and/ or noise in the process environment itself.

Through the proper design of a system, the process can be made insensitive to variations, thus avoiding the costly eventualities of rejection and/ or rework. In order to determine and subsequently minimize the effect of factors that cause variation, the design cycle is divided into three phases of System Design, Parameter Design and Tolerance Design.

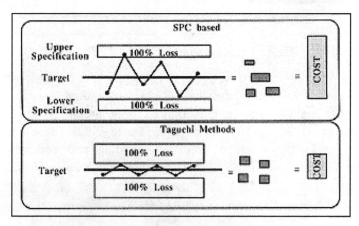

Figure **23:** A Comparison of Methodologies

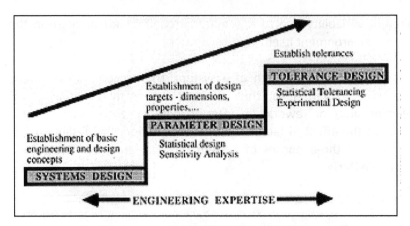

Figure 24: Stages in the Design Cycle

It should be mentioned that the application of Taguchi methods to plastics and composites processing has been attempted by a number of investigators (Warner and O'Connor 1989; Steele et al. 1988; Dockum et al. 1990; Karbhari et al. 1992; Slotte 1992). These include applications in the areas of injection molding and compression molding, as well as in structural reaction injection molding (SRIM) and RIM.

*****

Chapter 6 - Analysis of Variance

In statistics, ANalysis Of VAriance (ANOVA) is a collection of statistical models and their associated procedures, in which the observed variance is partitioned into components due to different explanatory variables. The initial techniques of the analysis of variance were developed by the statistician and geneticist R. A. Fisher in the 1920s and 1930s and are also sometimes known as Fisher's ANOVA or Fisher's analysis of variance, due to the use of Fisher's F-distribution as part of the test of statistical significance.

6.1 Overview

There are three conceptual classes of such models:

- Fixed-effects model assumes that the data come from normal population, which may differ only in their means. (Model 1)
- Random-effects model assumes that the data describe a hierarchy of different population whose differences are constrained by the hierarchy. (Model 2)
- Mixed effects model describes the situations where both fixed and random effects are present. (Model 3)

In practice, there are several types of ANOVA depending on the number of treatments and the way they are applied to the subjects in the experiment:

- One-way ANOVA is used to test for differences among three or more independent groups.
- One-way ANOVA for repeated measures is used when the subjects are subjected to repeated measures; this means that the same subjects are used for each treatment. It may be noted that this method can be subject to carryover effects.

- Factorial ANOVA is used when the experimenter wants to study the effects of two or more treatment variables. The most commonly used type of factorial ANOVA is the 2 × 2 (read as: two by two) design, where there are two independent variables and each variable has two levels or distinct values. Factorial ANOVA can also be multi-level such as 3×3, etc. or higher order such as 2 × 2 × 2, etc., but analyses with higher numbers of factors are rarely done because the calculations are lengthy and the results are hard to interpret.
- When one wishes to test two or more independent groups subjecting the subjects to repeated measures, one may perform a factorial mixed-design ANOVA, in which one factor is independent and the other is repeated measures. This is a type of mixed effect model.
- Multivariate analysis of variance (MANOVA) is used when there is more than one dependent variable.

6.2 Models

There are multiple models of analysis, out of which highly used ones are discussed below.

6.2.1   Fixed-effects model

The fixed-effects model of analysis of variance applies to situations in which the experimenter has subjected the experimental material to several treatments, each of which affects only the mean of the underlying normal distribution of the "response variable".

6.2.2   Random-effects model

Random effects models are used when the treatments are not fixed. This occurs when the various treatments (also known as factor levels) are sampled from a larger population. Because the treatments themselves are random variables, some assumptions and the method of contrasting the treatments differ from ANOVA model 1.

Most random-effects or mixed-effects models are not concerned with making inferences concerning the particular sampled factors. For example, consider a large manufacturing plant in which many machines are used to produce the same product. The statistician studying this plant would have very little interest in comparing the three particular machines to each other. Rather, inferences that can be made for *all* machines are of interest, such as their variability and the overall mean.

6.3 Logic of ANOVA

Partitioning of the sum of squares

The fundamental technique is a partitioning of the total sum of squares into components related to the effects used in the model. For example, we show the model for a simplified ANOVA with one type of treatment at different levels.

$$SS_{Total} = SS_{Error} + SS_{Treatments}$$

The number of degrees of freedom (abbreviated *df*) can be partitioned in a similar way and specifies the chi-square distribution which describes the associated sums of squares.

$$df_{Total} = df_{Error} + df_{Treatments}$$

The F-test

The F-test is used for comparisons of the components of the total deviation. For example, in one-way or single-factor ANOVA, statistical significance is tested for by comparing the F test statistic

$$F^* = \frac{MSTR}{MSE}$$

Where:

$$MSTR = \frac{SSTR}{I - 1}, \ I = \text{number of treatments}$$

And

$$MSE = \frac{SSE}{n_T - I}, \ n_T = \text{total number of cases}$$

to the F-distribution with $I - 1$, n_T degrees of freedom.

Using the F-distribution is a natural candidate because the test statistic is the quotient of two mean sums of squares which have a chi-square distribution.

6.4 ANOVA on ranks

As first suggested by Conover and Iman in 1981, in many cases when the data do not meet the assumptions of ANOVA, one can replace each original data value by its rank from 1 for the smallest to N for the largest, then run a standard ANOVA calculation on the rank-transformed data. "Where no equivalent nonparametric methods have yet been developed such as for the two-way design, rank transformation results in tests which are more robust to non-normality and resistant to outliers and non-constant variance, than is ANOVA without the transformation. However it was noticed that the rank transformation of Conover and Iman (1981) is not appropriate for testing interactions among effects in a factorial design as it can cause an increase in Type I error (alpha error). Furthermore, if both main factors are significant there is little power to detect interactions.

*****

Chapter 7 - The Library of Orthogonal Arrays

Orthogonal Array (OA) generation can be learned easily. It is very unlikely that, besides the straightforward array generation of the full factorial case, by attempts the tester will succeed in generating an orthogonal array of more than 4 factors. Complex algorithms are needed for this. As of today, the most common algorithms for generating orthogonal arrays of strength 2, are discussed below. This needs high level mathematical and statistical knowledge to understand.

1. Rao Hamming algorithm
2. Difference Schemes algorithm
3. Hadamard matrix family of algorithms
4. Transformation from symmetric to mixed arrays.

7.1 Rao Hamming algorithm

The name is shared by two outstanding scientists who independently and for essentially different problems found basically the same algorithm. The concept underlying Rao Hamming algorithm is really simple. If the below picture is looked into:

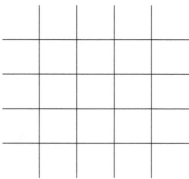

Figure 25: The concept of Rao Hamming algorithm

It represents **two parallel pencils** of straight lines in the plane. They intersect in **16** points, because only **4** straight lines have been singled out from the pencils. If a symbol or label is put to identify the straight lines in the pencils, each point can be labeled with the couple of symbols of the intersecting straight lines in the point: it is a kind of a Cartesian coordinate system. This is also a 16 runs orthogonal array of strength *2* with only 2 factors with 4 levels given by the labels of the intersecting lines in the 2 pencils. It has to be noted that:

- A factor is a pencil of straight lines,
- A level is the symbol which identifies a straight line in the pencil,
- A run is a point of intersection and has levels as coordinates.

Now the point becomes more complex. Instead of an Euclidean (infinite) geometry, a finite *geometry* is considered. A finite geometry is not defined on real numbers, infinite as they are, but on **finite fields**, called Galois fields from the name of the illustrious French genius Evariste Galois. He died when he was 21 years old. Imagine how much could he have gifted mathematics with astonishing findings if he would have lived long!

In the example, $GF[2^2]$, would be used, that is the (Galois) finite field with 4 (2^2) elements (0, 1, α_1, α_2).

The field to be chosen is determined by the number of levels that can be represented as the power 2.

$GF[2^2]$ is a field because it can be shown that it has both an addition and multiplication operations with corresponding operation tables and with the basic property of no '0' divisors. The product is '0' if and only if at least 1 of the 2 factors entering the product is 0. The common arithmetic can thus be performed. It is possible to show that, provided 's' is a prime power p^k, p being a prime number, a unique GF[s] exists, besides isomorphisms.

Because 4 is a prime power number, with p = 2, it can be added and multiplied with the elements in GF[2^2] as in a common numeric field using proper addition and multiplication tables. If a finite geometry of dimensions 2 from GF[2^2] is now built, it is easy to show that it is made up of just 16 points. It is also possible to show that in it there are 5 pencils of parallel straight lines. A straight line has to be interpreted as an algebraic one, where the only thing of interest is a linear formula equaled to 0.

For instance, $u_0 + u_1 * x_1 + u_2 * x_2 = 0$

In some textbooks it could be found a slightly different formula for a straight line, namely $u_0 x_0 + u_1 * x_1 + u_2 * x_2 = 0$

because it is easier to use projective coordinates in finite geometries.

We will use the first (affine) representation, because the second one brings into play the flat at infinity which can seem a bit clumsy for the initial reading.

The 'direction' of the straight line, that is the parallel pencil where the straight line lies, is given by the couple (u_1, u_2) of co-efficients. We have 16 cases, which reduce to 15 as soon as the (0, 0) couple is excluded. Moreover proportional co-efficients lead to the same pencil. Only 3 co-efficients of proportionality are admissible in the set (0, 1, α_1, α_2) because 0 would bring everything to 0. And hence we come to 15/3 = 5 parallel pencils.

It can be noted that different parallel pencils intersect in a way that each straight line of the first pencil intersects all the straight lines of the other one, just as in the figure. Each pencil contains 4 distinct straight lines corresponding to u_0 moving in the list $(0, 1, \alpha_1, \alpha_2)$: 20 straight lines in all. Within each pencil, there are 4 straight lines and they can be labeled as $(0, 1, \alpha_1, \alpha_2)$.

Now by the correspondence between factor and pencil, there is the possibility of allocating 5 factors. Each pencil has 4 straight lines whose labels will become the levels of the factor at the point of intersection. Each couple of pencils can be kept as a two dimensional Cartesian coordinate system for the finite geometry we are talking about. The design appears simply as the coordinate value of each run along all candidate pencils as coordinate axis: 5 in all.

The Rao Hamming algorithm can be used anytime when the number of levels s $=p^k$ as a prime power.

Arrays of Rao Hamming construction have the general form:

$$OA(s^n, (s^n-1)/(s-1), s, 2)$$

where
- s^n is the number of runs
- s is the number of levels
- 2 is the strength
- n is the dimension of the geometry.

For instance, OA(8, 7, 2, 2) or, in our notation, S_OA_8_2p7 is a 3 dimensional geometry because $8=2^3$.

Here are some examples:

- The already mentioned OA(8, 7, 2, 2) which is found in the library labeled as S_OA_8_2p7_RH with 8 runs, 7 factors all at 2 levels.

- OA(16, 5, 4, 2) which is found in the library labeled as S_OA_16_4p5_RH with 16 runs, 5 factors all at 4 levels.
- OA(27, 13, 3, 2) which is found in the library labeled as S_OA_27_3p13_RH with 27 runs, 13 factors all at 3 levels.
- OA(64, 21, 4, 2) which is found in the library labeled as S_OA_64_4p21_RH with 64 runs, 21 factors all at 4 levels.
- OA(64, 63, 2, 2) which is found in the library labeled as S_OA_64_2p63_RH with 64 runs, 63 factors all at 2 levels.
- OA(81, 40, 3, 2), etc.

If we look at the OA(8, 7, 2, 2) design - now $8=2^3$. Which kind of Galois field is used? The number of levelsis 2. Hence it is operated in the (smallest) Galois Field $GF[2^1]$, but the finite geometry has three dimensions, the exponent of 2 for getting 8. Because we have 3 dimensions in the geometry, each point is the intersection of 3 planes instead of 2 straight lines. The number of different pencils of planes in the geometry is 7. Then the equation for a plane would be:

$u_0 + u_1x_1 + u_2x_2 + u_3x_3 = 0$
with u0, u1, ..., u3 and x1, ..., x3 all taking values in (0,1).

The possible directions in the plane are 7, excluding the combination (0, 0, 0) for u_1, ..., u_3. In this case, the only admissible proportionality factor is 1.

The array OA(27, 13, 3, 2) is built in the 3 dimensional space over the finite filed $GF[3^1]$. There are 27 different points corresponding to 27 runs as intersections of 3 planes in 13 pencils.

The equation of a plane is again $u_0 + u_1x_1 + u_2x_2 + u_3x_3 = 0$.

But now u_0, u_1, ..., u_3 and x_1, ..., x_3 all take values in (0, 1, 2). The number of pencils is (27 - 1)/(2 - 1) because there are 27 different combinations for u_1, u_2, u_3 disregarding the (0, 0, 0) one and 2 proportionality factors leading to the same direction.

7.2 Difference Schemes algorithm

Difference schemes (DS) are tables of rows and columns with s symbols such that the difference between each pair of columns yields all the symbols 1, 2, …, s.

If a difference scheme is available, an orthogonal array can easily be generated simply replicating the difference scheme 's' times and adding to each replication all symbols in turn modulo(s): if the sum exceeds 's', divide by 's and keep the remainder.
Hence the problem becomes finding difference schemes. For instance, the multiplicative group of a Galois field is a difference scheme.

An example is

0	0	0	0
0	1	2	3
0	2	3	1
0	4	1	2

as the multiplication table of $GF[2^2]$.

Many difference schemes have been discovered through the years. Of course only small difference schemes are useful in conjoint applications.

Unfortunately no general algorithm has been found and it seems that group theoretical approach could provide some help. Abelian groups are a good resource for the creation of Difference

Schemes.

Besides a plain addition modulo s, more complex combinations are possible for getting orthogonal arrays from Difference Schemes. Here are some, just for the sake of example.

- The Kronecker product of suitable OA's and DS's is again an OA. By clever selection of ingredients OA's and DS's, it is possible to generate many mixed arrays.
- The Kronecker product of suitable Difference Schemes is again a Difference Scheme
- Bose and Bush recursive construction combines recursively a number of DS's.

Let us consider the below Difference Scheme:

0	0	0	0	0	0
0	1	2	1	2	0
0	2	1	1	0	2
0	2	2	0	1	1
0	0	1	2	2	1
0	1	0	2	1	2

It has 3 symbols (0, 1, 2). By the simple "add modulos" rule an array of 18 runs with 6 factors each at three levels is generated. It can be improved adding something more. Also a very important mixed array can be derived by a suitable transformation rule (Wang and Wu mixed array).

7.3 Hadamard matrix family of algorithms

A Hadamard matrix is a DS with only two symbols: -1, +1. The interest in Hadamard matrices lies in the Hadamard conjecture which states that all multiple of 4 have a corresponding Hadamard matrix. Hadamard matrix are square matrix with a fixed column of just 1's.

The smallest one is

$$H_2 = \begin{matrix} 1 & 1 \\ 1 & -1 \end{matrix}$$

H_4 does not differ from the Rao Hamming S_OA_4_2p3_RH, H_4 =

1	1	1	1
1	-1	1	-1
1	1	-1	-1
1	-1	-1	1

after the removal of the first column which corresponds to the intercept and a symbol recoding.

Not all Hadamard matrices can be generated by the Rao Hamming algorithm just by the addition of a column of 1's. Rao Hamming works, if the number of levels is a power of a prime number. And this happens in a Hadamard matrix, where the number of levels is 2 (prime number). But not all Rao Hamming arrays are square after the addition of a single column of 1's. Moreover, the number of rows in a Rao Hamming OA is a power of the number of levels.

Let us recollect the general form OA[s^n, $(s^n - 1)/(s - 1)$, s, 2]

Hadamard matrices are square and the number of rows in the array need only to be a multiple of 4 (conjecture). For instance, 12 is a multiple of 4, it is not a prime power being the product 3 * 4. No Rao Hamming construction would yield a H_{12} matrix.

The array S_OA_12_2p11_HD is a symmetric array with 12 runs and 11 factors all at two levels plus the column with all 1's corresponding to the intercept of the model. The only way to generate it is by Hadamard construction techniques. They are more than one and, usually, very difficult. Even the Hadamard conjecture is still undecided.

A useful finding in generating a new Hadamard matrix from two known ones is:

The Kronecker product of 2 Hadamard matrices of order a, b is a Hadamard matrix of order (a x b).

We can start from small matrices and get new ones in a kind of chain rule. Starting from H_2, we can get in a straightforward way:

- $H_4 = H_2 \otimes H_2$
- $H_8 = H_2 \otimes H_4$
- $H_{16} = H_4 \otimes H_4 = H_2 \otimes H_8$

H_{16} is a variant of the Rao Hamming array S_OA_16_2p15_RH.

This progression of Kronecker products with 2^m rows is also known as Sylvester type matrix series.

H_{20}, the Hadamard matrix of order 20, cannot be generated this way, because 20 is not a power of 2 and would be "jumped" in the progression of Kronecker products just explained. It is generated by the Williamson method of circulant matrices.

The point to be kept in mind is that Hadamard matrices fill up some gap left over by Rao Hamming algorithm while duplicating entries.

7.4 Transformation from symmetric to mixed arrays

A small array can be substituted for a single factor with as many levels as there are runs in the small array.

For instance, form an S_OA_16_4p5¬_RH a M_OA_16_4p4_2p3_RH is got by putting the complete S_OA_4_2p3_RH inside a column of the array.

In this way we can get:

- M_OA_16_4p4_2p3_RH
- M_OA_16_4p3_2p6_RH
- M_OA_16_4p2_2p9_RH
- M_OA_16_4p1_2p12_RH
- M_OA_16_2p15_RH

The last one can be also generated in a finite 4 dimensions geometry on the Galois field $GF[2^1]$.

It can be noted that all these arrays give birth to a design matrix with the same number of degrees of columns and then of degrees of freedom. It is enough to remember that a *4* level factor is hosted in three columns in the design matrix.

We thus have:

- 4 factors at 4 levels + 3 factors at 2 levels: 15 degrees of freedom;
- 3 factors at 4 levels + 6 factors at 2 levels: 15 degrees of freedom;
- 2 factors at 4 levels + 9 factors at 2 levels: 15 degrees of freedom;
- 1 factors at 4 levels + 12 factors at 2 levels: 15 degrees of freedom;
- 15 factors at 2 levels: 15 degrees of freedom.

All these arrays support the correct modeling of the corresponding problem.

More complex transformations can be applied to larger designs. If an 8 level factor is available it can host an 8 run array with 7 factors at 2 levels in place of the factor at 8 levels. Mixed transformations can be applied to a design where some 4 level factor coexist with some 8 level ones.

*****

Chapter 8 – Six Sigma – An Introduction

Since lot many processes/ testing have been discussed above regarding quality, it was thought that Six Sigma, which is an important methodology for process improvement to achieve quality can be introduced.

Six Sigma (6σ) is a high-performance and metric-driven methodology, conceptualized in the early 1980s for "breakthrough improvements" in processes and product design, leading to reduction in defects resulting in higher monetary benefits and customer delight. Six Sigma success stories involve drastic improvements in the bottom-line by designing and monitoring everyday business activities that minimize waste and resources while increasing customer satisfaction. This methodology has been successfully implemented in many companies as diverse as Allied Signal, Ford, General Electric, Honda, Motorola, Raytheon, Sony, Texas Instruments, etc. and has become a way of life for countless others.

Six Sigma incorporates a pivotal process to aggressively pursue a campaign that boosts customer satisfaction, increases capability, improves profitability and generates higher yields. Six Sigma involves the use of statistical tools within a structured methodology for gaining the knowledge required to deliver products and services that are better and more cost effective than what the competition is offering. This quantified and objective process enables faster and easier decision making. The list of tools and techniques encapsulated in Six Sigma may be similar to other approaches, however the methodological framework into which they fit and the overall structure of a Six Sigma effort distinguish it from other approaches.

Six Sigma methodology is prescriptive in nature, applicable to all processes and products, detailing 'how' the activities are to be performed. It involves building customer-centric processes from an outside-in perspective.

Methodologies

Two popular Six Sigma methodologies are:

- DMAIC (**D**efine-**M**easure-**A**nalyze-**I**mprove-**C**ontrol): applicable for improving the **existing processes**, products or services
- DMADV (**D**efine-**M**easure-**A**nalyze-**D**esign-**V**alidate): applicable for designing and developing **new** products, processes or services; also called as DFSS (Design For Six Sigma) methodology

Six Sigma is a rigorous and disciplined methodology that uses data and statistical analysis to measure and improve a company's operational performance. Six Sigma aims for virtually error free business performance by the identification and elimination of defects in manufacturing and service related processes.

In the early and mid-1980s engineers at Motorola decided that the traditional approach of measuring defects in thousands of opportunities was not good enough in order to meet customer expectations. Motorola was being consistently beaten in the competitive marketplace by foreign firms, which were able to produce better products at a lower cost. A case in point was the Quasar television sets, which Motorola used to manufacture in the United States. Due to poor quality production this business became unviable for Motorola and they sold off the business to the Japanese. Within a short period of time the same production facilities were turning out products with 1/20th of the number of defects they had produced under Motorola management. Eventually, even Motorola's own executives had to admit that "quality stinks".

Two Motorola engineers are thought to have pioneered the effort towards development of a new standard of measuring defects per million opportunities – Bill Smith and Mikel Harry; Bill Smith introduced the term "Six Sigma".

Sigma, σ, is a letter in the Greek alphabet used by statisticians to measure the variability in any process (standard deviation). The performance level of a process or product can be measured by measuring the variability of the process or product characteristics. This is done by calculating and using the Sigma Level of the process by analysis of data. The higher the Sigma Level, the better is the performance.

Processes in traditional companies typically operate at three or four sigma performance levels. In the course of operations these processes create between 6,200 and 67,000 defects given a million opportunities to do so. For traditional companies the non-value adding costs are typically in the range of 25 to 40 percent of their revenues. By stark contrast companies operating at six sigma levels of process maturity spend only around 5 percent of their revenues fixing problems that are non-value added to the customer.

Six Sigma is about helping an organization make more money. Six Sigma focuses on improving quality (i.e., reduce waste/ defects) by helping organizations produce products and services better, faster and cheaper. In other words, Six Sigma focuses on defect prevention, cycle time reduction and cost savings.

The savings attained as a percentage of revenue varies from company to company and are likely to vary from 1.2% to 4.5%. Some indicative figures on savings obtained by a number of companies over the last few years are presented below:

Table **24: S**avings obtained using Six Sigma

Company	Period	Revenue (US$ B)	Saving (US$ B)	% Revenue Saved
Motorola	1986 - 2001	357	16.0	4.5
Allied Signal	1998	15.1	0.5	3.3
General Electric	1996 - 1999	382.1	4.4	1.2
Honeywell	1998 – 2000	72.3	1.8	2.5
Ford	2000 - 2002	43.9	1.0	2.3

Approach

The broad approach for carrying out improvements can be summarized by the following diagram:

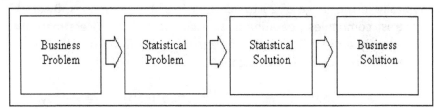

Figure **26:** Approach for Six Sigma

One starts with the business problem, gathers relevant data and transforms the problem to a statistical problem. Statistical tools and techniques are used to then arrive at the statistical solution to the problem and finally this solution leads to the real world business solution.

Six Sigma involves changing business processes organization wide; it is a means by which organizational change can be effected and its strategic goals achieved. This effort is implemented top-down with the CEO spearheading the effort. Improvements are driven in the form of improvement projects that typically have timelines running between 2 to 4 months. Each project has associated with it a set of associates who have varying degrees of involvement in the effort. An outline of the roles associated with improvement is presented below.

Master Black Belt

This is the highest level of proficiency in Six Sigma. Master Black Belts must know everything the Black Belts know, as well as understand the mathematical theory on which the statistical methods are based. They should be in a position to assist Black Belts in the application of Six Sigma tools and techniques in different business scenarios, including unusual situations. Master Black Belts usually propagate training on the Six Sigma body of knowledge organization wide and because of the nature of their duties, communications and teaching skills are as important as technical competence.

Black Belt

Candidates for Black Belt status are technically oriented and who are actively involved in the process of organizational change and development. Candidates may come from a wide range of disciplines and need not be formally trained statisticians or engineers. However, they are expected to master a variety of statistical tools and techniques. Black Belts assist Green Belts during the course of improvement projects.

Green Belt

Green Belts are trained on Six Sigma methodology. These associates lead improvement projects and should be capable of forming and facilitating Six Sigma teams and managing Six Sigma projects from start to finish. Green Belts are expected to complete at least one improvement project successfully soon after being trained on Six Sigma.

*****

Appendix 1 - Glossary

Active experiment	When the experimenter intentionally varies the inputs, then the experiment is active.
Blocking	This is the procedure by which experimental units are grouped into homogeneous clusters in an attempt to improve the comparison of treatments by randomly allocating the treatments within each cluster or 'block'.
Completely Randomized Design	The structure of the experiment in a completely randomized design is assumed to be such that the treatments are allocated to the experimental units completely at random.
Defect	If the value observed from on output during an experiment and the expected values of the output are different, then it is called an error, defect or discrepancy.
Design	The way in which variables are intentionally varied over many runs in an experiment.
Design of Experiments (DoE)	Active experimentation, done under controlled conditions in a logical structured manner, is a tremendously powerful tool and the type of experimentation is called DoE.
Discrepancy	See Defect
Error	See Defect
Experimental Design	Everyone is concerned with the analysis of data generated from an experiment. It is wise to take time and effort to organize the experiment properly to ensure that the right type of data and enough of it, is available to answer the questions of interest as clearly and efficiently as possible. This process is

	called experimental design. The specific questions that the experiment is intended to answer must be clearly identified before carrying out the experiment. We should also attempt to identify known or expected sources of variability in the experimental units since one of the main aims of a designed experiment is to reduce the effect of these sources of variability on the answers to questions of interest. That is, we design the experiment in order to improve the precision of our answers.
Experiments	An act that is performed to document the behaviour of the processes corresponding to each of the inputs.
Factor	A factor of an experiment is a controlled independent variable; a variable whose levels are set by the experimenter. A factor is a general type or category of treatments. Different treatments constitute different levels of a factor. For example, three different groups of runners are subjected to different training methods. The runners are the experimental units, the training methods, the treatments, where the three types of training methods constitute three levels of the factor 'type of training'.
Factorial Design	A factorial design is used to evaluate two or more factors simultaneously. The treatments are combinations of levels of the factors. The advantages of factorial designs over one-factor-at-a-time experiments are that they are more efficient and they allow interactions to be detected.
Factors	See Variables

Interaction	An interaction is the variation among the differences between means for different levels of one factor over different levels of the other factor.
	Example
	A cholesterol reduction clinic has two diets and one exercise regime. It was found that exercise alone was effective and diet alone was effective in reducing cholesterol levels (main effect of exercise and main effect of diet). Also, for those patients who did not exercise, the two diets worked equally well (main effect of diet); those who followed diet A and exercised got the benefits of both (main effect of diet A and main effect of exercise). However, it was found that those patients who followed diet B and exercised got the benefits of both plus a bonus, an interaction effect (main effect of diet B, main effect of exercise plus an interaction effect).
Interactions	When the effect of one variable on the response depends on the level of another variable, it is called an interaction.
Levels	Each variable in an experiment has its own unique settings referred to as levels or treatments.
Main Effect	This is the simple effect of a factor on a dependent variable. It is the effect of the factor alone averaged across the levels of other factors.
	Example
	A cholesterol reduction clinic has two diets and one exercise regime. It was found that exercise alone was effective and diet alone was effective in reducing

	cholesterol levels (main effect of exercise and main effect of diet). Also, for those patients who did not exercise, the two diets worked equally well (main effect of diet); those who followed diet A and exercised got the benefits of both (main effect of diet A and main effect of exercise). However, it was found that those patients who followed diet B and exercised got the benefits of both plus a bonus, an interaction effect (main effect of diet B, main effect of exercise plus an interaction effect).
Model	Mathematical description of how the response behaves as a function of the variable(s).
One Way Analysis of Variance	The one way analysis of variance allows us to compare several groups of observations, all of which are independent but possibly with a different mean for each group. A test of great importance is whether or not all the means are equal. The observations all arise from one of several different groups (or have been exposed to one of several different treatments in an experiment). We are classifying 'one-way' according to the group or treatment.
Passive experiment	When the experimenter merely observes the system and records any changes that occur in the inputs and the corresponding outputs, the experiment is passive.
Predictors	See Variables
Process	Processes have inputs that determine how the process operates and outputs that are produced by the process.
Randomization	Randomization is the process by which experimental units (the basic objects upon which the study or

	experiment is carried out) are allocated to treatments; that is, by a random process and not by any subjective and hence possibly biased approach. The treatments should be allocated to units in such a way that each treatment is equally likely to be applied to each unit. Randomization is preferred since alternatives may lead to biased results. The main point is that randomization tends to produce groups for study that are comparable in unknown as well as known factors likely to influence the outcome, apart from the actual treatment under study. The analysis of variance F tests assume that treatments have been applied randomly.
Randomized Complete Block Design	The randomized complete block design is a design in which the subjects are matched according to a variable which the experimenter wishes to control. The subjects are put into groups (blocks) of the same size as the number of treatments. The members of each block are then randomly assigned to different treatment groups. Example A researcher is carrying out a study of the effectiveness of four different skin creams for the treatment of a certain skin disease. He has eighty subjects and plans to divide them into 4 treatment groups of twenty subjects each. Using a randomized blocks design, the subjects are assessed and put in blocks of four according to how severe their skin

	condition is; the four most severe cases are the first block, the next four most severe cases are the second block and so on to the twentieth block. The four members of each block are then randomly assigned, one to each of the four treatment groups.
Responses	The outputs of the processes.
Treatment	In experiments, a treatment is something that researchers administer to experimental units. For example, a corn field is divided into four, each part is 'treated' with a different fertilizer to see which produces the most corn; a teacher practices different teaching methods on different groups in her class to see which yields the best results; a doctor treats a patient with a skin condition with different creams to see which is most effective. Treatments are administered to experimental units by 'level', where level implies amount or magnitude. For example, if the experimental units were given 5mg, 10mg, 15mg of a medication, those amounts would be three levels of the treatment. 'Level' is also used for categorical variables, such as Drugs A, B and C, where the three are different kinds of drug, not different amounts of the same thing.
Two Way Analysis of Variance	Two Way Analysis of Variance is a way of studying the effects of two factors separately (their main effects) and (sometimes) together (their interaction effect).
Variables or factors or predictors	The inputs to the processes.

Appendix 2 - List of Abbreviations

#	Abbreviation	Expansion
1.	API	Application Program Interface
2.	ANOVA	ANalysis Of VAriance
3.	BVA	Boundary Value Analysis
4.	CEO	Chief Executive Officer
5.	DFSS	Design For Six Sigma
6.	DMADV	**D**efine-**M**easure-**A**nalyze-**D**esign-**V**alidate
7.	DMAIC	**D**efine-**M**easure-**A**nalyze-**I**mprove-**C**ontrol
8.	DS	Difference schemes
9.	DoE	Design of Experiments
10.	ETL	Extract, Transform and Load
11.	FTP	File Transfer Protocol
12.	IEEE	Institute for Electrical and Electronic Engineers
13.	IT	Information Technology
14.	JMP	Statistical Software widely used
15.	MANOVA	Multivariate Analysis Of VAriance
16.	OA	Orthogonal Array
17.	OVAT	One Variable At a Time
18.		structural reaction injection molding (SRIM) and RTM
19.	RSM	Response Surface Method
20.	RIM	Reaction injection molding
21.	SDLC	Software Development Life Cycle
22.	SLA	Service Level Agreements
23.	SPC	Statistical Process Control
24.	SRIM	Structural Reaction Injection Molding
25.	SS_E	Sum of squared errors.
26.	SS_R	Regression sum of squares
27.	SS_T	Total sum of squares
28.	UAT	User Acceptance Testing

*****

Appendix 3 - List of Figures

Appendix 4 - List of Tables

Bibliography

Though primarily our experience and usage of OA was the prime factor for writing this book, lot many books and web-sites have also been referred to make it a structure. They are:

1. http://syque.com/
2. http://www.pmi.org.
3. Exploratory testing explained; James Bach.
4. Phadke, Madhav S. Design of Experiment for Software testing.
5. S. Hedayat, John Stufken and Guoqin Su. On the construction and existence of Orthogonal Arrays with three levels and indice 1 & 2.
6. Angela Dean, Daniel Voss. Design and Analysis of Experiments.
7. Robert.F.Brewer. Design of Experiments for Process Improvement and Quality assurance.
8. Pressman, Roger S. Software engineering a practitioner's approach.
9. Sloane, N. J. A. A Library of Orthogonal Array.
10. Berger, Bernie. Efficient Testing with All-Pairs.
11. Farook, Omar, J, Padmasankar and KP, Sanju. Application of Design of Experiments in Software Testing.
12. Sankar, Unni and Thampy, Deepa. Applying Taguchi Methods in Software Product Engineering.

*****

About the authors
Ramamurthy N

Ramamurthy is a versatile personality having experience and expertise in various areas of Banking, related IT solutions, Information Security, IT Audit, Vedas, Samskrit and so on.

His thirst for continuous learning does not subside even at the age of late fifties. He is also pursuing research on Information Technology and Samskrit and has submitted his dissertation for Ph.D. degree. He is into a project of developing a Samskrit based compiler.

It is his passion to spread his knowledge and experience through conducting classes, training programmes and writing books.

He has already published books:

His other books are being published:

 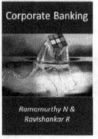  

Books being penned: Corporate Finance, Banking – GRC, Information Security in Banks, Devee Mahatmeeyam, Devee Baagavatam, Breath to live and more

Let us all wish him to continue his service in spreading his knowledge.

*****

Ravishankar R

Ravi is currently working in Accenture as a **SAP Treasury/ FSCM consultant**, with experience working in delivery, capability building, Solutioning & pre sales area. He is an expert in the area of SAP FSCM/FICO.

He has published whitepapers, developed various PoCs, conducted training programs and created differentiators in niche areas of SAP ERP.

He is an active and **top contributing** member of **SAP Developer Network** (SDN) in the area of **Treasury applications**. He has completed Production Engineering from National Institute of Technology, Trichy with top honors.

*****